DIGITAL
TRAILBLAZER

Harness Technology and Marketing
To Rapidly Grow Your Business

RICHARD WOODS

RETHINK PRESS

First published in Great Britain 2015

by Rethink Press (www.rethinkpress.com)

© Copyright Richard Woods

Cover image © dollarphotoclub/adidesigner23/

CONTENTS

To
Cara, Mylo and Bump,
Mum and Dad,
Tim and Jenny,
and our amazing Yomplings, past and present.

INTRODUCTION

Welcome, Prospective TrailBlazer

I am delighted to meet you at the start of your exploration into becoming a Digital TrailBlazer.

Digital TrailBlazing is a fast track road to dizzy new heights for you and your business. It is fun, challenging, and most of all rewarding.

This book gives you eye-opening strategies that are so easily implemented you will kick yourself for not doing it earlier. There are sections that require more time and effort, and of course nobody climbed Everest on their own, so be ready to assemble a Summit Team around you.

But be prepared: Digital TrailBlazing is not for the faint-hearted. If large turnovers give you vertigo, if becoming web-famous worries you, if taking on sales enquiries by the bucket load gives you cold feet, I totally respect that and would *not* recommend you read on.

However, if you like the idea of sitting on top of a mountain of growth that nobody thought you would achieve; if you like proving doubters wrong and making the people closest to you overwhelmed with pride, then strap on your best pair of hiking boots because it's about to get remarkable for you!

What is a Digital TrailBlazer?

A Digital TrailBlazer is a business or individual who harnesses the power of the internet and technology to rapidly grow their business.

TrailBlazing businesses are everywhere, initiating the untravelled routes in their industry, energetically going where most do not dare to venture.

A Digital TrailBlazer promises themselves that being good is just not good enough.

OK is not OK.

Fine should be fined!

They are admired by many and put fear into their competition.

Digital TrailBlazers escape vanilla and go for triple chocolate chip with a flake.

Whether you are starting your journey or have an established business; whether you are starting from scratch or have tried a number of strategies to accelerate growth, you need to know that TrailBlazing is not about *trying* things. It is about lassoing a tried and tested ride to rapid, competition beating, mind blowing growth.

It's about creating a business that can afford you the time and income to achieve the things you want from life.

That is what I will show you in this book.

Who am I?

My name is Richard Woods and I am a Digital TrailBlazer.

Since graduating from university in 2005, I and my brother Tim have joined forces and built a number of great businesses by harnessing the power of technology and the internet.

We run a large portfolio of companies and investments, including an award winning digital marketing agency, Yomp Marketing; a corporate video, audio and photography business, Yomp VAP; over 50 independent local services websites; and an oil industry distribution business, Top-Up Fuels. All these businesses and investments harness the power of online marketing and technology to supersize their growth, and our personal wealth with them.

Looking back, it was clear that Tim and I learned the foundations of business growing up in an entrepreneurial household. Our father grew his oil business (also with his brother), starting with a small paraffin delivery job selling the bottles door-to-door (like a milkman, but with paraffin for house heaters), into the largest independent home heating oil distributor in the UK, with over 250 staff and turning over half a billion pounds per annum.

He was nominated for both the Entrepreneur of the Year and the City Deal of the Year awards within his 40-year career.

His story was the typical humble-beginning-to-riches story and it was impossible not to be inspired by his drive and talents. He would always push my brother, sister and me to take our own initiative and would make us work for everything.

My mother also had a big role in inspiring us as kids: she would regularly take us to museums and exhibitions, which opened our minds, and on long drives she would play audio books in the car – but not the usual children's audio books, but business audio books!

I learned how Alan Sugar built Amstrad, how Anita Roddick built The Body Shop and how Richard Branson built the Virgin empire.

They all taught me to dream and to stay hungry. Inspired by Branson, I still want to own my Necker Island and this is a massive driver of my personal ambition. It is my screen saver, it is on my wall, I even research it during my down time.

In education, I fine-tuned my learning when I proudly studied Business with Entrepreneurship at University and received a first class honours for my final thesis 'Is there a link between Dyslexia and Entrepreneurship?'.

After graduating I set up a number of successful businesses to get to the portfolio size I am at today. In the process my companies and I have won high profile awards in the US and UK for our work in marketing and digital media.

During this journey I have been lucky enough to meet and work with a number of successful, busy entrepreneurs. Every time I met them I was impressed at how they kept sole focus on what they do well and the parts of their business they are passionate about.

This insight was the starting place for the Digital TrailBlazer process.

WHY YOUR BUSINESS SHOULD BE A DIGITAL TRAILBLAZER

Has reading the Introduction made you think that your business would benefit from becoming a Digital TrailBlazer? After working with many small and medium sized businesses, it has become clear to me that new and growing companies often lack a comprehensive business growth plan and process.

A growth strategy is absolutely crucial for all businesses, and at the heart of this plan are two key ingredients: sales and marketing. They underpin your businesses success, irrespective of the industry you operate in or your target clients.

When I meet new business owners, or even those who have been around the block, I often hear that they have tried a few sales techniques and marketing channels but not received the results they desired. Many of them tell me that after trying something new for a month or two and getting dismal results they stop trying new types of marketing altogether.

This viewpoint is typical of small businesses nervous of getting burned by trying anything new, but as the well-known phrase goes:

> 'If you keep on doing what you've always done,
> you will always get what you always got.'

During the recent recession, many business owners I encountered would have been delighted if that quote had even been true for the marketing they conducted. Many small businesses started to see their classic marketing channels, such as the *Yellow Pages* or newspaper advertising, bringing far fewer responses and therefore shrinking the size of their business – *so they did not even get, what they had always got!*

This was due to both a decreasing number of new enquiries and their existing customers being poached by internet-savvy competition (the Digital TrailBlazers).

For entrepreneur clients, I conduct a full audit on their business, including the marketing channels they have tried, how these have been implemented and whether their performance has been effectively tracked.

I asked one accountant who had seen his business take a big hit and shrink from 18 staff to seven how he tracked the effectiveness of his Google AdWords campaign (pay-per-click adverts). He said that he had decided to stop this form of marketing because it was costing him too much for little return.

I probed further as I was interested in understanding how he knew it produced a low return. He told me that his team asked anyone who contacted the business how they had heard of it and their answer would normally be 'a friend has mentioned the firm' or 'through the website'.

I asked him what other work he does to drive people to the website.

He had registered his business with a number of online directories with links back to his website, employed a Search Engine Optimisation (SEO) company, sent out a newsletter every three months, set up a few social media profiles that he sent updates through, and created the AdWords campaign. Altogether, he was spending £2,300 per month on marketing activity that drove people to his website.

So I had to ask, 'How do you know that, out of the 14 enquiries you received the previous month, they were not all from Google AdWords?'

'Nobody said they had come from AdWords.'

Nobody had said that they found him through search engines or a directory either, so why did he not stop marketing through those platforms?

From my experience, when a sales lead is asked 'How did you hear about us?' they will never divulge the *full* route to how they found you. Why would they? They are on the phone to you now, and that's all that matters to them.

This example demonstrates one of the founding principles of the Digital TrailBlazer system.

Acknowledge and commit to tracking absolutely every marketing channel fully.

This way nobody slips through your tracking net and you know *exactly* which marketing channels are working for you and which are not, so budgetary decisions can be made based on data, not a gut feeling.

After a few more questions, it became clear that this accountancy practice had a lot to offer their clients but they were not telling their story in a compelling, interesting or provoking manner.

Looking at the business through fresh eyes started to expose issues in some of the new channels the owner had been trying. For example, a social media marketing supplier who was engaged to send four tweets a day proved to be doing this in a totally untargeted and untracked fashion.

For example, would you make contact with a business, hoping to be their client, in response to a tweet like this?

'It looks like it's going to be a sunny day today in London Town #happyworkday'

Or a 'call to action' tweet of this kind:

'For all your accounting needs, visit our website
www.theaccountantswebsitelink.com'

Let's face it, nobody is sitting there waiting for an unengaging, boring, not to mention blatant advert. Being a Digital TrailBlazer is about upping our online game if we want to grow our businesses and that also means the people around you too.

As the entrepreneur you cannot work upon everything, nor should you try too, so making sure your key team members are on their game is also vital.

Digital TrailBlazers understand that the key to successful sales and marketing is to implement a joined-up, dynamic process into their business; one that informs, delights and adds value to potential customers before selling to them.

By following the structure in this book, you too can delight your prospects into becoming your next clients.

There has never been a better time to harness the power of Digital Marketing

The world is ready for you to become an online sensation. There are over 3 billion internet users, all consuming information, buying products, using services and making connections. You already know this, but you probably also know that you have not harnessed the power of online marketing as well as you should have.

Everyone in the world has the ability to become an international TrailBlazing sensation. All you need is access to a computer and an internet connection. Think about the 18 to 20 year olds at universities around the globe. This very second a new competitor of yours is about to graduate into this digital world. This is the world they've grown up in, the world they've been educated in, and soon it will be the world they make their fortunes in.

They are coming to your world, they are about to join your industry, your market, your customers, your competitors. Now is not the time to panic, in fact quite the contrary: now is the time to welcome them from the top of your market, helping them up, harnessing their enthusiasm as well as making them your customer or supplier, not your competition.

It is inevitable that new wave after new wave of highly skilled and digitally savvy young people will crash into the shores of your carefully crafted business, but don't see this as a bad thing; this constant innovation and outside influence will help you to be better, to continue to ride this unstoppable wave and ride it high, as a TrailBlazer.

Digital TrailBlazers know that they have expert status, they may know about it now, or they are about to discover it. They also know they have a message and a high standard of conducting business which customers and potential customers alike will benefit from.

The Digital TrailBlazer system I cover in this book, will not only help you implement tried-and-tested marketing techniques that are tailored to your target customer, but you will also be able to track everything, aware at all times of exactly which marketing channels are producing results, increasing your return on investment and bringing new customers to you.

But first, as a Digital TrailBlazer, you need to know where the mission target is for your business. Where are you climbing to? What does the top of the mountain look like?

The Business Growth Mountain

Let me set the scene...

You are deep in the misty foothills of your mountain range. The only way to go from here is up. There is no turning back. You know what life back there is like and you will not suffer it anymore. Enough is enough: now is your time.

But where to go from here? Which turn do you take next? Do you have a map? Have you packed the right equipment? Is your team capable of supporting your ascent?

After years of dreaming about it and seven weeks of climbing, Edmund Hillary and Tenzing Norgay reached the top of Mount Everest, the highest mountain in the world, at 11:30 a.m. on 29th May 1953.

They were the first people to ever reach the summit.

Mount Everest had long been considered unclimbable by some and the ultimate climbing challenge by others.

Climbing Mount Everest is of course extremely dangerous and challenging: besides the freezing weather and the obvious potential for long falls from cliffs into deep crevasses, climbers of Mount Everest suffer from the effects of the extreme high altitude, often called 'mountain sickness'. The high altitude prevents the human body from getting enough oxygen to the brain, causing hypoxia.

All climbers of Mount Everest suffer from headaches, cloudiness of thought, lack of sleep, loss of appetite, and fatigue. – It happens to the best of them.

Overcoming challenges both mentally and physically to achieve your goals will sound familiar to many high achieving entrepreneurs. But the brave few who allow themselves to get acclimatised to their new altitude in business gradually become used to it, then they start to move faster and higher and higher, until one day they hit their business growth summit and the immense sense of pride and achievement takes all the pain, sleepless nights and worry away.

This may be how you feel at points along the way when climbing your own business growth mountain. Growth is scary, harnessing the power of digital can be hair-raising, investing in growth can take you so far out of your comfort zone that you get 'financial hypoxia' and turn back before reaching your goals.

Maybe that's why many businesses settle for rambling in the foothills rather than climbing in the mountain ranges.

This is why it can take climbers and business owners time to climb their Everest. It is why pauses along the way to make camp, assess the MAP (**M**assive **A**ction **P**lan), have a morale-boosting camp fire chat, rally the troops, and ready everyone for the next leg of the ascent, are vital.

There are many challenges with growing a successful business, but sometimes the biggest challenge of all is finding your own business growth mountain and making sure it is your Everest.

Never settle for climbing in the business foothills for too long.

What is your Everest?

Your Mount Everest is the business growth mountain that you never thought you would climb; the turnover that you did not think your business would achieve; the profit per month that your family and friends said was not possible; the turnover that you can only dream about as you read your umpteenth biography on a successful millionaire business owner.

It might be to turn over one million pounds a year; it might be to make five million pounds profit in a year; it might even be to turn over a billion. Whatever it may be, it will be unique to you and I will help you to make it achievable and realistic. Perhaps you have already listened to the doubters and have been put off the ascent to aspire only to lower hills that give you small satisfactions and wins. But this is not your Everest. Or even your first Everest. I believe a small business should climb its Everest every year!

As a business achieves the summit it should immediately be looking at the next one – and the next one will be even bigger than the last, but it will still be Everest. Each new Everest can only be the highest mountain in the world, once you have climbed the previous year's Everest. It's a never ending, ever growing mountain range.

Business is challenging, like climbing Everest.

So are you ready to get started?

Great, then let's look at the five key stages of a Digital TrailBlazers ascent.

The Digital TrailBlazer 5 Key Stages

I'm going to introduce you to a set of unique ideas, methodologies and tools to help formulate your strategy and fast track implementation.

They are contained in the Digital TrailBlazer 5-Stage Process

The process is based on my experience of working with many small businesses and validated with a range of high profile and highly successful entrepreneurs.

One thing these top business owners have in common is their intense focus on what they do well and the parts of their business they are passionate about. Each of them then outsources, automates and holds accountable the departments, suppliers and individuals who are responsible for helping their business to grow by achieving excellent measured results.

Every year, a successful business stands at the foot of their Businesses Growth Mountain, looking up and asking 'How do I get my turnover and profitability to the top of that mountain?'

Do I have a map?

Have I packed the right equipment?

Is my team capable of assisting my climb?

Do I even know what the summit looks like?

Harnessing the power of Digital and becoming a TrailBlazer answers these questions by using business growth processes, online marketing dominance, automation and return on investment (ROI) tracking.

To start with, a Digital TrailBlazer conducts a focused *BaseCamp* strategy session to plan their ascent to the top of their mountain, even if from here the summit is shrouded in cloud. This clearly shows them the size of the task ahead and what the obstacles are likely to be. They make sure they have the right team around them and have packed the correct equipment. Most importantly, they put their Massive Action Plan (MAP) together with a clearly planned route to the summit.

They set off through the foothills by targeting the quick returns from *Selling More to Existing Customers*. They do this by using the tried and tested techniques outlined in this book to find the under-served value within their current customer base and sell into that gap.

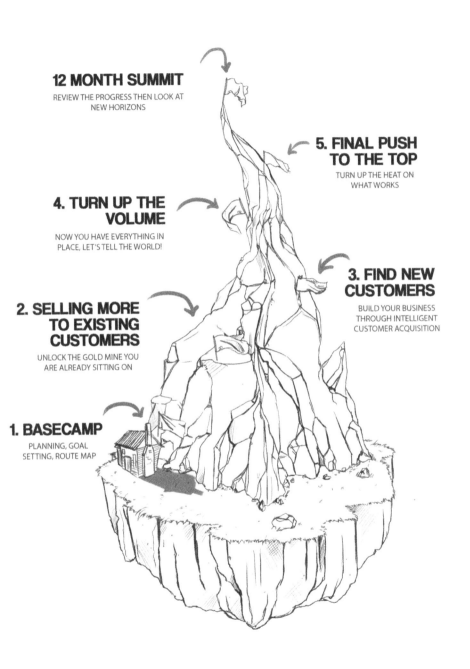

12 MONTH SUMMIT
REVIEW THE PROGRESS THEN LOOK AT
NEW HORIZONS

**5. FINAL PUSH
TO THE TOP**
TURN UP THE HEAT ON
WHAT WORKS

**4. TURN UP THE
VOLUME**
NOW YOU HAVE EVERYTHING IN
PLACE, LET'S TELL THE WORLD!

**3. FIND NEW
CUSTOMERS**
BUILD YOUR BUSINESS
THROUGH INTELLIGENT
CUSTOMER ACQUISITION

**2. SELLING MORE
TO EXISTING
CUSTOMERS**
UNLOCK THE GOLD MINE YOU
ARE ALREADY SITTING ON

1. BASECAMP
PLANNING, GOAL
SETTING, ROUTE MAP

Then a Digital TrailBlazer *Finds New Customers* by observing why their best, most profitable customers like them so much, and with this knowledge they set off to find other businesses that match their customer profile. Once found, they demonstrate why they are such a good fit and the value they can deliver. This part of the process grows the volume of perfect clients for a TrailBlazer's business and therefore their turnover and profitability in the process.

With the locked-in knowledge, skills and processes to find prospects, and when they become customers to sell more to them, the time is then right to *Turn up the Volume*. Digital TrailBlazers moving into this stage aim to be a click or two away from engaging with the perfect client online. They make their business a magnet for customers, partnerships, press and opportunity. They stretch further and louder to make growth viral for their business.

Once they have the first four key elements in place, Digital TrailBlazers pause to assess all the measurements, targets and activity. They also give their team a heart-felt motivational speech and drive forward, because they know it is time for the *Final Push to the Top*. This is where they tweak and perfect the past four stages, turning up the volume even further on the successes and pausing the less fruitful channels to make sure the whole of their business and processes run like a well-oiled machine.

They then drive forward to reach their campaign turnover target: *the top of their business growth mountain,* where it is time to celebrate in style.

Are you ready to join the TrailBlazers?

THE TRAILBLAZER JOURNEY

CHECK POINT 1 – BASECAMP

Our goals can only be reached through a vehicle
of a plan, in which we must fervently believe, and
upon which we must vigorously act. There is no
other route to success.

PABLO PICASSO

Other than humans, not many creatures or plants can live in high altitudes. This means that food sources for climbers of Mount Everest are relatively nonexistent.

In preparation for their ascent, climbers and their teams must plan, procure and then carry all their food and supplies with them up the mountain. Most summit teams hire Sherpas to guide them and help carry their supplies. Sherpas are a previously nomadic people who live near Mount Everest and have the unusual ability of being able to quickly physically adapt to higher altitudes, and are therefore natural guides and local assistants to explorers.

As TrailBlazers we take inspiration from the early explorers and make sure we have the right equipment and team on board to make our journey a success. This is why a business should revisit BaseCamp every year before embarking upon its 12-month climb.

BaseCamp is all about planning, structure and understanding the trail ahead.

Remember, without having a clear idea of where you are headed, how will you ever get there?

Where are you right now?

To find out, let's start by learning all about your business, then we can start to refine it into a TrailBlazing machine. This process is designed to get you in the right frame of mind to start planning your journey.

EXERCISE

Grab a pen and answer these questions as fully and honestly as possible:

How do the current financials look?
  Your last month Profit and Loss statement (P&L)
  Your last quarter P&L
  Your last 12 months P&L

What is your personal financial position?
  How much do you need per month to cover all bills and expenses?
  What is your disposable income?
  How much do you save into an investment account each month?
  What other investments do you have outside the business or product you are looking to grow?

Based on your answers to these questions, now create your key goals for the next 12 months:

Where do you want to be in 12 months?
Desired turnover
Desired profitability
Desired personal takings from the business

Answering these questions at the start of every year will surprise you and help to have a strong understanding of your business: Where are you now? Where are you headed?

To download a free *Where are you now?* worksheet, with bonus questions and planning tools, go to **www.digitaltrailblazer.co.uk/mastery**

Your Trail-MAP – a TrailBlazer's Massive Action Plan

'Stopping advertising to save money is like stopping your watch to save time.'
HENRY FORD

It is vital to set your 12-month goals, as outlined in the last exercise, ahead of completing your Trail-MAP.

Creating your business growth Trail-MAP works like creating an annual budget for your business.

Launching into a 12-month climb without carefully analysing the financial prospects in advance would be foolhardy for even the most seasoned TrailBlazers.

It is important to understand that even though becoming a Digital TrailBlazer heavily emphasises marketing and sales, this is not enough on its own to create a highly profitable business.

The act of budgeting by creating your Trail-MAP forces you to think through all the important numbers and to develop a picture of what your business is going to look like in 12 months. It will enable you to develop and maintain a thorough understanding of the internal financial workings of your business, your team requirements and capacity for growth. It really is a powerful business tool that will help you make better decisions when out on your mountain.

When preparing it, remember that it should:

Cover 12 months of business operation.

Use spreadsheet programs like Excel to enable you to revise and update quickly.

Comprise a complete 12-month Trail-MAP before starting the annual climb

Be reviewed, revised and if necessary updated every month

The Trail-MAP overview contains five major numbers for each month:

1. The projected sales and revenue for each month – The Turnover
2. The direct projected costs of delivering the Product/Service – The Cost of Sales
3. The projected costs of running the business other than the direct cost of sale – The Expenses

4. The profit or loss from delivering the Product/Service – The Gross Profit

5. The total profit or loss when both the expenses and Cost of Sales are deducted from the Turnover – The Net Profit.

The most important number is the top line – the estimated sales for each of the 12 months. This monthly number should be based upon the 12-month turnover goal you have just written down and realistically dividing it into monthly targets so by the final month you have achieve your goal.

You need to think about your current position and how increasing marketing investment month-on-month will in turn increase your monthly turnover figure.

EXERCISE

Take a spreadsheet and put 12 months across the top. In the first row beneath add the realistic turnover targets for each month. In the second row, add each month's Cost of Sale; in the third, Expenses; fourth is Gross Profit; and finally Net Profit for each month.

For a detailed example and an Excel spreadsheet template go to the TrailBlazer Mastery kitbag at **www.digitaltrailblazer.co.uk/mastery**

Your sales and revenue projections should be based on experience, your 12-month target, your lead generation abilities and business capacity.

The next part of your Trail-MAP should include all the costs of operation involved in producing and delivering the product or service to customers. These include:

The costs of purchasing or producing
the product or service

Sales and marketing costs

Your business's administration and operation costs

All fixed, variable and semi-variable
costs of business operation

Your final number should include 100% of all
out-of-pocket expenses necessary to achieve
your estimated sales revenues

The next part of your Trail-MAP is the total profit or loss from operations for that month. There will sometimes be months of the year where your business loses money. In a new business start-up, the first few months will usually show losses. The general sales and profit trends are most important.

Lastly, your Trail-MAP should reflect the cumulative profits or losses of the company over a period of months. The figures are brought together to get a total, these totals tell you when your business will break even and begin earning a profit. The total months where losses occur will tell you how much money you will have to borrow or provide to the business before it is profitable. An accurate budget should reveal the truth about your business's potential to reach the 12-month mountain top you set yourself at the start.

Remember, there is no point tackling an unrealistic mountain.

Achieving a realistic summit is better than getting lost on a mountain you should not have started climbing in the first place. Everest claims 15 climbers on average per year; think about this when reviewing that 12-month summit. Business is even less kind, claiming 50% of businesses in the first five years, so be honest and as accurate as possible.

Now we have our Trail-MAP, each major number should be reviewed each month. You should compare the actual results in each category against the projected results. Just the act of studying each number each month will improve performance in that area.

To help with this, share the Trail MAP with your accountant and ask them to review it with you each month, to see if you are on budget. This accountability could be priceless and very motivating.

As TrailBlazers we invest the time in BaseCamp to prepare an accurate MAP as we understand that ultimately it saves enormous amounts of time and money and often many months of wasted effort climbing in the wrong directions.

Your Current Marketing Assets

When you have completed your Trail-MAP, you will probably find yourself in a position where you need to increase your turnover month-on-month quite rapidly to hit the targets you set yourself at the start of BaseCamp. To achieve this we need to understand what is driving new business enquiries for you now, work on optimising your existing marketing channels and add new ones.

Having a number of marketing channels that work consistently well for your business is of great value. If you were to sell your businesses tomorrow, being able to prove that you have systems and processes in place that regularly generate the enquiries that feed your sales will increase its value.

Therefore, a fully functioning marketing campaign is an asset. To find out if you have these types of assets in place, let's look at how your current marketing is working.

Start by listing out your current marketing channels. These include *everything* you and your business does to market your products or services. That could be anything from business networking or exhibiting at trade shows all the way through to Twitter, a YouTube channel or writing a book.

Following the guide below, open a spreadsheet and name it as the month you are working on. Put the marketing channels down the left hand side, creating a row for each. Along the top add seven columns, which will judge the effectiveness of each marketing channel. Here's an example:

July		1	2	3	4	5	6	7
Marketing Channel		Web Hits	Web Leads	Email Leads	Tel Leads	Total Leads	Cost of Campaign	Cost per Lead
PPC								
SEO								
Promotional Gifts								
Essex Microsite								
Kent Newspaper								
Kent Microsite								
London Microsite								

The seven columns along the top are:

Web Hits – This is the number of visitors you get through the marketing channel per month. Later we will discuss setting up landing pages and micro websites for all marketing channels so that we can get an accurate figure for offline marketing such as trade shows, but for now if you only have the traffic levels for your main website, add that under the SEO column as this will be the organic traffic your website receives.

Web Leads – This is the number of website forms that have been filled in on the different websites and webpages you have that relate to that marketing channel.

Email Leads – This is the number of email enquiries you receive from each marketing channel.

Tel Leads – This is the number of phone calls you receive from the dedicated telephone tracking number you have in place for that one marketing channel. Don't worry if you do not have these in place. We will go through this later in BaseCamp.

Total Leads – This is the sum total of all the leads listed above

Now we have the start of our spreadsheet set up with every marketing channel, let's review how each element is performing.

In Total Leads, put how many enquiries in total per month you receive from each channel. If the channel is a trade show or a one-off event that does not feature in that month, list it but put a 0 in terms of cost and leads. This way you can still see that there are channels that give you short term gains, and you can pull these figures forward into an end of year review using a separate spreadsheet that calculates the totals each month.

Do not forget to list little marketing activities, such as one-off events or sponsorships. Fiddling around with these small numbers may seem crazy, but the concept is to be totally honest with yourself on the spreadsheet and give credit where credit is due. If that charity auction you attend once a year gives you two solid business leads, then put it down, as the event clearly deserves the credit and for one nice evening out that is a good return. Perhaps even it should be done more often?

Cost of Campaign – Now let's add in the numbers and spice things up a little bit more. Firstly enter the monthly cost of each marketing channel. There may well be channels that do not cost money directly, but try to make sure associates costs are linked, such as yours or a staff member's time to attend an event, the cost of travelling, or the time taken each day to use Twitter vs not doing something else, etc.

Make sure you divide all the non-regular costs associated with each channel by twelve to find the monthly figure and add them to the spreadsheet. For example, if you paid for your website in one hit, make sure you divide that investment by twelve months. Your spreadsheet should show a 'totals' strip running across the bottom. Dose that total costs per month figures look correct? What is missing? Make sure you are happy that each figure is not over or underestimated.

Cost per lead – Using the spreadsheet, divide the cost of each channel by the amount of leads, to find the cost of each lead. If you have a 0 next to the leads, put the full price of the channel into the column so as to demonstrate how much you are paying to get nothing in return.

Total Campaign Cost per Lead (Return on Investment) – Time for one of the most important figures, the return upon your time and monetary investment. To find this figure deduct the total cost from the total leads for the month, leaving you with a return on your investment figure.

Over the years I have worked with clients using this system. Many of the businesses have thought that they are doing a superb job, driving hundreds of enquiries and converting a good percentage of them into sales. When we have put these figures together we have often found that many marketing channels they had almost written off have a better return than the main channels they were investing in. This review and deep dive has allowed us to simply switch budgets from the underperforming channels into the performing channels, and the business's profitability and turnover grew overnight.

You may well find the same happening for your business.

I remember one particular oil distribution client who started their journey to become a Digital TrailBlazer the same year they had just spent £72,000 on *Yellow Pages* (printed book directories) and *Yell.com* (online business directory). As they had already committed to a year of advertising with Yell, we tracked this all the way though and soon realised that only six out of the 48 book directories they were in produced a return on investment. The others brought in very little, in fact many did not make enough sales to even cover the cost of advertising. We also realised that the *Yell.com* premium listing which ranked the company as number one within their area, only produced one or two more sales a month. Therefore, as the cost of the premium listing was far higher than a normal listing, the return on investment from the higher lead generation was lower than the normal listings.

The spreadsheets showed some remarkable data and as a result we were able to confidently take the £72,000 spent year one with Yell and re-invest £30,000 the following year into other marketing channels that we knew were working for them, such as leaflet mailshots, email marketing and search engine optimisation (SEO). We then saved £20,000 straight to the bottom line: as Yell had inflated their budget year-on-year, it was making the total marketing way out of proportion with turnover and therefore the business became instantly more profitable.

Finally, we kept the other channels running with Yell which kept the relationship between our client and Yell, but on an even playing field totally based around win/win and return on investment.

To this day they remain using Yell, but only as and where it works.

Bring it all together

A fully working spreadsheet like the one below should be totally enlightening; it gives you everything you need to really make some big decisions in your business.

July	1	2	3	4	5	6	7
Marketing Channel	Web Hits	Web Leads	Email Leads	Tel Leads	Total Leads	Cost of Campaign	Cost per Lead
PPC	1,673	16	9	9	34	£798.00	£23.47
SEO	3,068	27	11	39	77	£850.00	£11.04
Promotional Gifts	98	4	0	6	10	£250.00	£25.00
Essex Microsite	271	1	0	23	24	£125.00	£5.21
Kent Newspaper	139	0	0	2	2	£280.00	£140.00
Kent Microsite	76	0	0	4	4	£125.00	£31.25
London Microsite	65	0	0	9	9	£125.00	£13.89
Total	5,390	48	20	92	160	£2,553.80	£35.75
Total Campaign Cost Per Lead							£15.96

Completed correctly, it will create illuminating reading. From the first time you produce this spreadsheet before you set off from BaseCamp, to the month you summit your Everest, it is good practice to update it every month you are out on your climb. It will put the control in your hands to make buying decisions against lead generation, plus it will hold your staff and suppliers accountable to the most important output of marketing – lead generation.

Do not worry if you are unable to add all the data the first time you create the spreadsheet. Setting up lead generation tracking is the bread and butter of what you are about to learn in BaseCamp. By the time you set off up your mountain you will have packed all the tools you need to fill in this spreadsheet entirely.

Free Template

To download a free copy of the TrailBlazer ROI Report Template as an excel spreadsheet, go to
www.digitaltrailblazer.co.uk/mastery

TrailBlazer Mastery

For Master TrailBlazers using an end-to-end sales and marketing client relationship management system (CRM), you will be able to report exactly the names of the leads, their source marketing channel and what they have spent to date. This is a good time to pull those figures from the system for review. For more information on CRMs check out the TrailBlazer Mastery kitbag at
www.digitaltrailblazer.co.uk/mastery

Which target audience will get you to your summit quickest?

One of the most important decisions we can make when sitting in our BaseCamp hut at the foot of our business growth mountain, is to confidently commit to focusing on profitability when choosing the correct target audience for our business.

This allows everything else that arises from that decision to be laser targeted in its strategy for optimising sales and marketing resources towards this target audience. So you will not be wasting time and money chasing many different customer groups or offering umpteen types of service variation.

When identifying the most profitable target market you need to look at your current client base and segment out the clients who:

Receive the most value from your services and will therefore pay a premium price for them

Are large enough to afford that premium price

Generate the least amount of problems / expense when you are serving them

Once you have the list of clients who share these three common values, you will be able to draw even more common traits from them. Are they in similar industries, are they a certain size, do they buy certain services and not others?

Try to group the results by the following sets of questions:

1. For business to business sales (B2B) what businesses are you targeting?
   Industry
   Type of business
   Size of business
   Number of staff

2. For business to consumer (B2C) and also complete for the decision maker for (B2B)
   Occupation
   Age range
   Gender
   Affluence

Applying this analysis will then allow you to think about the profitability of the type of businesses you want to target.

It is also important to consider the lifetime value of the customer, so note what they would spend in one year, three years and five years.

A good example of someone targeting profitable clients is Jayne, a speech pathologist, who used to work with hospital patients and university students who needed speech therapy.

Through conversations with contacts in the business world, Jayne found a much more lucrative market niche: foreign business executives who needed help with accent reduction to improve their speech and presentation skills. These executives were willing to pay top dollar for her services because outstanding communication skills were key to their success.

The foreign business executives were also more cost-effective to serve. Jayne created a program for accent reduction, which she easily adapted for each new client.

Once Jayne identified this more profitable market, it became much easier to generate new business. The foreign business executives had natural and tightly knit networks through their expatriate communities and they often referred Jayne to their friends and colleagues. Word of Jayne's services spread quickly, generating more business from high paying clients and, therefore, higher profits for Jayne.

When you target an audience like Jayne did, finding your unique selling point and creating an effective marketing strategy is much easier. In the next section you will find out how to discover your unique selling point to target the audience you have just selected.

What is your unique selling point?

A unique selling point (USP) is what makes your business stand out from the crowd and tells your customers what is special about you.

Having a clearly defined point of difference from your competition will help exponentially, as you develop your marketing and start pitching your business to current and potential clients in CheckPoints 1, 2 and 3.

Your target market is swamped with advertising messages every day; they simply become numb to it and cannot re-evaluate services and products every time they need to make a purchase.

Human brains like to group things together when they are trying to make buying decisions, as it is easier to draw comparisons between service offerings.

For example, if you are going on holiday you may select a luxury hotel by comparing all hotels that have been given a five star rating. In comparison you might try to find a budget hotel by comparing all hotels that are priced under £65 per night.

Finding your unique selling point is about first knowing which group you belong to, then expressing why you are unique within that category. Trying to be a total maverick and different from any other competitor and market is desperately difficult and can leave you isolated, with consumers not easily understanding your offering.

Knowing that people are already buying within your group, within its market, will allow for you to quickly grow and gain sales by standing out within the group parameters.

To find your group, ask yourself why does your target audience purchase items from the market you are operating in?

What needs does that market meet for them? Are they looking for a time-saving, cost-saving, luxury experience, a trust-worthy supplier or something else?

Try asking customers, colleagues and friends so that you can make a list of all the reasons why someone might choose to buy the services you and your competitors are offering.

Now we know how and why your customers are grouping you and your competition together, let's find out what your competitive advantage is.

Make a list of all the customer needs your service could / does meet. They could be lowest cost, simplest to work with, most local, fastest response, biggest capacity, the best portfolio. These attributes are all potential USPs for your business.

Compare these USPs against your competitors' service offerings and remove the USPs that are already being well covered by others. You are looking for a unique selling point, so it is ok to still offer these solutions to your customer's needs, but we want to find that point of difference from your competitors and therefore the gap in the market your business sits within.

For each USP that is left, carefully think about it and make sure it does align with what you realistically want your business to grow into. Do you really want to be the cheapest? Do you really want to be open 24/7? Do you really want to offer weekly client meetings? Whatever your USPs are, make sure you are happy to build your business and brand around them.

Next, take the surviving USPs and write a couple of paragraphs around them. Why are they unique from the competition? Why are they important to the customer? How do they fulfil the need the customer has?

Go out to your target audience and simply ask them to read the paragraphs around each one and put them in order of what matters the most to them. Make sure the amount of people you ask are in double figures otherwise the pool of opinions will be too small.

Finally, double check that you have the right USP. Does it have a strong benefit? Is it memorable? Is it clear who your business is targeting? Can you deliver what it promises? Is it actually unique, or could a competitor claim the same thing?

Now use this positioning as we start to climb the business growth mountain. It should be driving the development of your TrailBlazer strategy from this point on, whether you are creating a website, a social media campaign or just talking to your current clients and reminding them why they chose you in the first place.

Let's Start Packing

Now we know how effective your current marketing channels are, where you want to be in twelve months and which audience is going to help get you there. We can now create the key elements that will assist your climb.

There are two important categories your business needs in its backpack while climbing your business growth mountain.

These are – The Three Trail-Trackers, The Three Digital Assets.

Let's understand why they are so important.

The Three TrailTrackers

A quotation caught my eye nearly 10 years ago when I was at university. It was from an American department store owner called John Wanamaker. He said:

> Half my advertising works,
> I just don't know which half

At the time I was completing my dissertation on small business entrepreneurship for which I interviewed many small business owners. I found that most of them did not know which marketing channel was the most effective, and 10 years later 80% of the clients that come through my marketing agency's door are still none the wiser.

Early TrailBlazer – John Wanamaker
Born: July 11, 1838
Died: December 12, 1922

Main Location: Philadelphia, Pennsylvania, USA
US department store owner who championed the use of
left field marketing techniques, such as:

Full-page newspaper advertisements
Ad-covered horse-drawn carriages
Sign-carrying pedestrians known as sandwich men
The creation of the first restaurant in a general store
First to send buyers overseas for a foreign market study
Free public choral concerts
Free displays of artwork
Children's Christmas drawing contests

A true TrailBlazer of his generation and someone that
we all can take inspiration from.

Inspiration from Wanamaker combined with my drive to create a business growth product that gives entrepreneurs 100% clarity. I set about putting three methods together to track the returns from marketing spend, which become the key figures to see what works and what does not. The end result is a top level view of where money is spent and what to continue with and what to stop.

From months of testing I found the following combination of tools essential to give 100% clarity:

1. Website Forms and InfoSwap Process
2. Telephone Tracking Numbers
3. Website Analytics

Trail-Tracker #1 – Website Forms and InfoSwap Process

Website forms are vital to all service sector businesses that use the power of online marketing to grow. A website form will be what is used to generate an enquiry for your business. Unlike product based businesses that have ecommerce websites where people can buy things (such as Amazon), a service-based company needs to generate business enquiries to then sell their services to the prospect.

Digital TrailBlazers do this through the *InfoSwap Process*.

What is an InfoSwap?

An InfoSwap is online currency in the service sector world.

As a supplier of a service you are the holder of specialist information in your industry. Yes you are! How long have you been doing what you're doing? You are an expert in what you do, otherwise why would anyone engage your services?

So you the expert needs to publish something that your target audience want and will value. This might be a how-to-guide, service demo or an online tutorial. This piece of online content is available for all to access as long as they do one simple thing…

Leave their name and a method of contact (usually telephone number and email) so you can see how they got on.

Once a website visitor does this, we consider it a *lead* and therefore a potential client. You then phone the lead and convert it into an appointment, event attendee, or directly into a sale.

This then is what we consider a *conversion*.

Seems simple enough, right?

The fact is, 80% of companies do not take enough advantage of this way of building a database of interested, targeted, motivated potential clients.

The potential uses for InfoSwaps are almost limitless, but using the process I will outline next, here are some great examples of how you can use it to generate leads or sales:

InfoSwap Lead Generation Ideas

Download an e-book you have written as a deep dive into your subject matter

Subscribe to a newsletter with monthly articles and tips

Industry report with facts and statistics

41

A Subscribe Now page to your blog or news feed, so they can get your content via email each time it is published

Purchase your product or service online.

Audio podcasts (works like your own radio station)

Register for a webinar: a live presentation
and interactive question and answer session

A *How To* process checklist, so people can do
something themselves

Register to get early access to an online course
or book release

Access to a video course you have created

To gain access to private Facebook or Linked-In groups

Become a customer of your online business

Buy your book

Understanding that all your online marketing channels should have InfoSwaps is the first step. Getting it right and creating something that works is the second, so here are techniques which help achieve InfoSwaps that work:

Create the buzz – Before a user is willing to complete an InfoSwap they have to recognise their need for the information you are offering to swap for their information. On-page videos, testimonials and a few short descriptive paragraphs will help you to achieve this. Try to identify a problem and present an InfoSwap that solves that problem. You also need to communicate the benefits of filling in the form and accessing the content: what will the user get out of content they are accessing?

Offer a little extra – Sometimes you may have to sweeten the deal to encourage users to complete a call to action. Incentives could include discounts, bonus material, entry into a competition or a free gift.

Limit each web page to one InfoSwap – Too many sign up forms become overwhelming. Studies using eye-tracking and online behaviour software have shown that if a user is presented with too many options they are less likely to select any of them. Limiting the number of choices to a yes/no decision makes a user more likely to sign up.

Compelling action button copy – An InfoSwap call to action button should clearly tell users what you want them to do. They should include active words such as: Call, Buy, Register, Subscribe. All of these encourage users to take an action.

Add urgency – To create a sense of urgency and a need to act now, the call to action description can include time-sensitive phrases such as: Offer expires March 31st, For a short time only, Register now and receive a free gift.

Position on the page – For optimum sign ups your InfoSwaps should be placed high on the page and in the main central column. If the InfoSwap relates to a specific section of copy, have it right at the end of that section, loud and proud across as much screen as possible. Top right also has merits for large pages of web copy, but more and more people are used to it being here and therefore it becomes part of the webpage we no longer see, like billboards that melt into the background of your morning commute. Misplace the form and users will not even acknowledge its existence.

Use negative space – The position of your call to action is not the only thing that matters. The space around it is also crucial. The more space around a call to action (negative space) the more attention is drawn to it. Clutter up your call to action with surrounding content and it will be lost in the overall noise of the page.

Use a stand out colour – Colour is an effective way of drawing attention to InfoSwaps, especially the call to action button. If the rest of the website uses a style sheet of only a few colours, go for a contrasting bright colour to draw the eye to the InfoSwap.

Less form fields is more – We want to contact the users who convert, but not get drawn into building up mountains of demographic information. Fewer fields categorically means more leads; it's human nature to be suspicious of anyone asking for too much information, plus it takes up your website users' time unnecessarily. Name, email, telephone – then ask yourself 'why would I need any more info than that?' if there is an excellent case for one or two more fields then go for it, but less is *very* much more on website forms.

Auto responders – Make sure you have an automatic email set up on all InfoSwaps with tailored information on that particular offer. Don't forget to thank them for taking the time to look further into your services.

Then what? – Consider what happens when a user does respond to your InfoSwap. The rest of the process needs to be as carefully thought through as the call to action itself. Who will be responsible for following up? What sales process will the lead go into? How will it be tagged on your customer relationship management software (CRM).

An effective InfoSwap is the cornerstone of all online assets. Get it right and it can generate real, measurable return on investment with business leads for your sales team to follow up on daily. Get it wrong and all your marketing investment to get users to your website could be wasted through missed opportunity.

So now we know what the theory is, what do you need to start tapping into this 24/7 lead generator?

You need content for the InfoSwap

Let's go back to when we found out you were in fact an expert.

Every person in business is able to help others through published content. This content can take many forms, for example an article, video, tick list, infographic, blog, podcast, etc. The list is endless; what is important is that you think about the best method to get your idea across and that you are capable of creating or engaging the services of someone to help you create it.

The content itself should be a subject that easily leads into one of the main services you offer. For example, if you are a recruitment agency you know that your customers may be interested in salary surveys within their niche, so they can make sure they are pitching their job at the correct level.

One of my clients created a very successful salary survey for UK marketing consultants which they hosted as the download on their website. They optimised the page for the keywords 'Marketing Consultant Recruitment UK'. This landed them both potential clients looking to recruit new candidates, and also potential candidates looking to change jobs who wanted to see how their current salary stacked up.

45

They simply filtered through all the downloads each day and matched the interested parties. They gained considerable business from that one InfoSwap.

Website Form

Here is the website form process we have used for many successful Digital TrailBlazers.

The idea is to create a website form that tracks the amount of enquires it receives easily and quickly. It should also distribute high quality auto responder emails both to the website user and to you so you can follow up the lead.

For a typical InfoSwap I recommended the form only has the following fields:

- Name
- Email
- Telephone

When the form has been completed two auto-responders should be sent:

Auto-responder 1 to the website visitor: a short email with branded header and footer and a simple 'Thank you for your enquiry' message in the middle. If the email also requires an attachment (the content that is being swapped) this should be small in size – no more than 10mbs and ideally under 1mb so that is does not get caught in mailbox spam filters.

Auto-responder 2 to you: so you can immediately put the enquiry into your sales process and start moving the lead into a customer.

This auto-responder should mention the lead source in the title, so that rules can be set within your inbox for storing, files in folders so that lead volume is easily tracked and the return on investment from each marketing channel can be monitored.

Website Form Thank You Page

After the auto-responders are sent, the website visitor is immediately forwarded to a Thank You page with a 'next steps' section. The next steps can be relevant website pages to the download, social media links, etc.

The Thank You page should also have the InfoSwap on it, such as the Downloadable PDF or embedded videos as well as it being attached to the auto-responder. This way the visitor will have two opportunities to get the document or access the content.

The Thank You page also needs to be set up as a goal within Google Analytics so 'Goal Tracking' there can also be seen. This figure will tell you how many people are downloading your InfoSwap (*more on this in Trail-Tracker #3 – Website Analytics*).

This process is vital to stop service businesses losing out on potential sales who are searching the internet for a business just like yours. A well put together InfoSwap will create a steady stream of potential customers for you to follow up on, and also a nice dataset to show the effectiveness of your online assets and marketing campaigns.

TRAILBLAZER MASTERY
INFOSWAP CRM INTEGRATION

I recommend for advanced Digital TrailBlazers that your Client Relationship Management software (CRM) is used to create the code for these forms, so that they can be integrated directly into your software. These CRMs will allow different form conversion lists and tags to be auto-generated and follow ups automatically created within the software.

The process this should follow, is as follows:

An anonymous website visitor will find a piece of engaging content upon your website and decides that they would like to read more about that content and therefore swap their information i.e. name, email and telephone number for the e-book (for example). Once the form is submitted they will receive an email with the e-book, as well as being diverted to a thank you page with the e-book available on it.

When this happens the visitors details will automatically be added to the Digital TrailBlazers CRM, a tag will be added to their record saying: 'what they have downloaded', 'from where they downloaded it' and 'what date and time they downloaded it'. As soon as this has happened the TrailBlazers CRM also has created a task for them or one of their team to call the prospect and have a discussion upon what they thought about the e-book.

This is the opportunity to make a sale or invite the prospect to meet with you to discuss their requirements further.

For more on this process and the CRM software I recommended, visit **www.digital-trailblazer.co.uk/mastery**

48

Trail-Tracker #2 – Tracking Telephone Numbers

Online marketing is one of the best ways to promote your business and offers excellent customer enquiry tracking facilities. However, a serious and often-overlooked flaw exists. Phone calls triggered by online marketing often go untracked, which undervalues their impact and effectiveness.

Usually businesses will publish the same phone numbers on their website as they do on their email marketing campaigns and their business cards, but if you get 100 calls a month from this number, which form of advertising is driving those enquiries?

Call tracking gives TrailBlazers the missing ingredient for a true marketing return on investment calculation.

How does it work? You acquire a set of new phone numbers and you direct the calls to them back to your existing phone line.

It's really easy to do. You do not have to change your phone line or your phone provider and your existing number still works as well.

Your existing phone rings in just the same way; you answer it in the same way. The only differences are that you have multiple numbers all routing back to the same number and you have placed a different number on each different marketing channel, so that now you know which advert or piece of marketing generated each call because you can go online and check instantly at any time. A typical online call tracking platform will tell you how many calls you've received and on which numbers.

Here is the common scenario for a typical service sector business:

Your staff do not have time to ask an inbound caller about how they found your business, because they're focused on helping the caller and closing sales. Even if they do ask, have you ever tried asking someone if they clicked an organic listing or a paid search ad? Callers usually do not understand what that means and you are in danger of putting the potential client off in the first seconds of your call. So placing a different call tracking number on each of your marketing channels and keeping it exclusive to that one cost centre will give you a goldmine of data.

Some of the more common features and benefits of call tracking include:

Total Calls – the number of calls will show you the effectiveness of the channel.

Length of Call – you can score leads based on call length and see which marketing channels generate the longest calls and therefore the quality of the lead.

Call Recordings – allow Digital TrailBlazers to learn more about their customers' needs and questions, which can be used to update site content, change product or service offerings and target specific marketing messages to them. Call recording also serves as an invaluable employee training opportunity, so you can work on how they handle each call.

Without actual call information like the data set above, it's easy for business owners to throw their hands up and say:

'Online marketing doesn't work, I spent all this money and only received one or two leads.'

Even if advertisers do know they're getting calls from their online activity, they don't know if it was the HQ website, their social media profiles or online directories, so they cannot properly optimise their campaigns and their focus online.

Let's say I run a mortgage broking business. I have placed three adverts in local newspapers, I have a website that I drive organic traffic to, I send a monthly email marketing promotion out and I have business cards that I leave at all the networking meetings I attend.

That makes six separate marketing channels that I currently operate and invest in:

1. Local Newspaper A
2. Local Newspaper B
3. Local Newspaper C
4. Website
5. Email Marketing
6. Business Cards

With Trail-Tracker #2, Tracking Telephone Numbers, I'll buy six separate phone numbers and I will allocate one phone number to each marketing channel. I'll keep my existing phone number, so any existing mortgage clients can still call on that number and not distort the statistics, but all the new numbers will ring on my same existing phone line. The software is clever enough to track all the separate call statistics going to the same place and over a month or two I will know exactly which marketing channels are working best for me.

It works like a dream and it's one of the most under-used tools available to businesses.

One thing that Digital TrailBlazer will notice is that most media companies are frightened of tracking numbers. The last thing the local newspapers or even your outsourced social media agency want is you being able to track precisely how many calls the adverts you place with them are generating, because that would make them accountable to lead generation. As a Digital TrailBlazer, make sure you invest in tracking numbers as everyone you work with will stay focused on the most important output of marketing – Lead Generation.

For all the reasons above and more, call tracking is the answer for TrailBlazers.

HOW DO YOU GET TRACKING NUMBERS SET UP?

There are several providers of Tracking Numbers, including Yomp Marketing. We have a platform running with thousands of numbers managed for our clients. Head over to **www.Digital-TrailBlazer.co.uk/toolkit** for the most up-to-date list of tracking number companies I have used and recommend.

Trail-Tracker #3 – Website Analytics

Knowing what is happening on your websites is vital when you are continually trying to improve them. There are many ways to see data about your website, but for Digital TrailBlazers the best place to start is Google Analytics.

Google Analytics is a web-based platform which allows you to collect data about the visitors who come to your website. It enables you to collect and analyse information about everything from how the user arrived at your website, what they did whilst on your website and whether or not they converted, as well as offering additional information about the user themselves.

The software is split into four key reporting areas:

Audience (who is visiting your site)

Acquisition (how they are getting to your site)

Behaviour (what they are doing on your site)

Conversions (have they completed what you wanted them to)

Collectively and individually, these give excellent insights when we want to optimise our marketing campaigns and target the correct audiences for our business.

Getting started is simple, all you need to do is set up an account with Google, enter your website's address (URL), and you will be given a piece of code to add to the footer of each of your webpages. The code is not seen by visitors but sits in the background sending data back to Google.

Your website guys can do this in seconds for you, or alternatively you can install plugins that do it for you if you are using software such as WordPress for your website.

Once you have Google Analytics all set up properly and you are seeing the basic data set of the volume of visitors and which pages they are visiting, you can then start to link up other Analytics tracking methods. One method is through Goal Tracking, which is an option found within Google Analytics. It automatically tracks pre-set goals each time a website visitor completes one.

As a service sector business, I would start with Goal Tracking the Thank You Page for your InfoSwaps, because each time a visitor finds the Thank You Page it means they have downloaded the related InfoSwap and therefore have become a *Lead*.

To set this up, take the webpage URL of the Thank You Page, for example **www.your-website-adress.co.uk/thank-you**, and add that into the Goals section of Google Analytics. Then for each page you can place a monetary Goal Value. This value is based upon the lead that is generated from that particular InfoSwap. So if you are an estate agent, you might have several different Thank You Pages and therefore goal values as a 'Property Lettings' lead will be a different value than a 'Property Sale' lead.

The way you work out the monetary value is by taking your average order size from clients who the InfoSwap is targeted at (for example £1,000 average order size), divide that number by the number of leads required to get a conversion (for example one in four leads = one sale) and you will find the Goal Value. The average order size of £1,000 divided by the four leads required to make one sale = £250 goal value.

Once you have this level of data you can then make strategic decisions by knowing who is using your website, what InfoSwaps work the best, and what monetary value your website is bringing you.

Together the Trail-Trackers are powerful tools that light up your path to summit success.

The Three Digital Marketing Assets

Now let's look at the Digital Marketing Assets that will help you to achieve the targets set within your Trail-MAP.

The three digital assets I am about to introduce you, have helped me grow my business exponentiall, and have also grown 100's of my clients businesses. You may think that some of the assets are obvious. You may already be using some of the assets yourself.

However, I rarely meet a business that uses all three effectively.

As a Digital TrailBlazer, if you put all of the three assets to work for your business you will see a beautiful flow of targeted business enquiries pouring into your inbox or down your phone line every month.

All three will be harnessing the power of the three Trail-Trackers. So if you are ready, let's strap on your digital hiking boots and find out what they are.

Asset #1 – The HQ Website

When starting out on any adventure, setting up a strong Head Quarters (HQ) is so important. The HQ is where everything reports to and where anyone interested in the expedition can find out anything and everything they want to know about you and your mission.

Digital TrailBlazers do this through their HQ website.

The HQ website is your company's main website. It should be the most highly worked upon asset in your armoury and of course the website address that goes onto your business cards, email signatures and anywhere else you can promote it.

Its purpose is to inform your target audience of everything your business does, what is happening in your world and how your target audience can be part of it.

If a web visitor leaves a website without leaving their contact details, that is of course not the web visitor's fault; they may or may not have obtained the information they needed but they obviously have not been enticed, drawn or motivated enough by the website owner to swap their details for information, a sample or a product.

If this happens, the business owner is losing most of the potential they have already worked so hard to attract.

As Digital TrailBlazers, we want to create high quality, enticing websites that move the audience to leave their details in exchange for some benefits they have received.

To create such a high quality HQ website, there are two key points to remember:

Great memorable design

When you meet a potential customer for the first time in person, you make sure you look smart, or are dressed in the appropriate way for your industry. However, for many business owners a website that meets a client with broken pages, poor design, and text seamlessly floating across a page is acceptable.

As a Digital TrailBlazer you need to make sure your website says something about you, not the tired-just-got-out-of-bed-on-a-Sunday-after-a-lively-Saturday-night version of you (charming as I am sure it is) but the best you. The you that is in flow and wants to shout from the roof tops about how great you are.

One of our earliest Digital TrailBlazers are entrepreneurial jewellers Simon and Nadine. When we first met I was taken aback by their creative and unbelievably welcoming personalities; they clearly made an amazing team working together, something many couples find extremely challenging, but they were a perfect combination of dynamic creativity and technical strategic thought.

The challenge they set us was to create an HQ site for them that said everything about their 'kooky', 'refined', 'non-tacky' Chiswick Jewellers. Their strategy for the site was one third product, one third communication, one third information.

What we eventually launched was a complete digitally painted masterpiece. Every element was hand drawn, painted, and then digitally enhanced into a virtual tour of the Jewellers. Books fly off the shelf and land open so the viewer can read about ethical diamond mines or the origins of gem stones. We installed a web camera system in store so a website visitor can have a one-to-one conversation with an expert. We also created dynamic ways of showing off all the products on hand-drawn display cabinets, with 360 degree turning video of each ring or necklaces, etc.

Website copy is so important

So picture this, you have the best made, best designed powerhouse of a website and on the first page there are three spelling mistakes. Some people (like me) would barely notice, but others (like my brother) would be horrified! Worse still, it would be the absolute end of any possible relationship with the company and website. Now I understand that this is extreme, but mistakes in written content are almost unforgivable to some people and, let's face it, it does give a really bad impression of your business.

The other important element to think about, is how you get your message across. As a Digital TrailBlazer you need to be engaging and exciting. Writing mundane content about general subjects will not excite your audience. Try to find a voice when you are writing website content, use bullet points, short paragraphs and try to run anecdotes and stories through your message.

Finally

When creating your HQ website, make sure all the Trail-Trackers are on it as it will be a big source of lead generation as we kick off search engine optimisation campaigns and raise your profile later in your TrailBlazer campaign. Also make sure that you keep it up to date and that you publish fresh articles and blog posts regularly. There is nothing worse than hearing about a great business or entrepreneur and then going onto their website and seeing outdated, badly spelled, badly designed content.

Approach your HQ as if you are having someone important turn up to read it front to back every day and never settle for OK as it needs to be excellent.

TRAILBLAZER MASTERY

There are many small parts that make up a really special HQ website, I have therefore put together a **99 Ingredients to a Perfect HQ Website** Recipe Sheet available at **www.Digital-TrailBlazer.co.uk/mastery**

Asset #2 - TrailBlazer OutPosts

As a Digital TrailBlazer you will notice that many of your products or services attract customers who have specialist requirements and/or are based in small geographic pockets. These customers can be extremely lucrative and totally underserved by you and your competition.

These are the opportunities that a TrailBlazer OutPost looks after for you.

An outpost for our Victorian mountain climbers were small camps of four or five explorers detached from the main exhibition team and stationed at a distance from the HQ, usually in very remote locations. The outpost's task was to understand a part of the wilderness and to liaise with any locals to gain knowledge and understanding of the area. They would report back to the main exhibition team with their findings, which would usually provide massive value to the whole mountain ascent.

As Digital TrailBlazers we harness the principle of these remote outposts to create small pockets of value for niche services or location-specific customers who will appreciate a local focus and the care taken to tailor content for their needs. In turn they will help us climb our business growth mountain by becoming new customers.

These TrailBlazer OutPosts take the form of keyword specific Micro Websites and are defined as:

Small, informative websites catering to a narrow niche of potential customers and seamlessly giving value (usually in the form of information or free samples) in exchange for permission for the information giver to start a conversation with them.

If you think about the mountain analogy, it's like a welcome shelter for your potential clients when they are out on their own business growth mountains. Let's say, they have been caught in a storm and need a good place to shelter, a warm fire and a hot cup of tea. In exchange you get to talk to them, understand their challenges and gain help in your own business growth ascent by having the opportunity to make them a customer.

To set up your Digital OutPost you need to start by thinking about your main products/services which customers typically contact you about on your HQ website: what keywords do they use, what do they enquire about, and what do they buy? That is List One.

Then write down which products/services you sell but do not receive enquires about through your marketing, or which you sell but you do not currently have any keyword rankings for. That is List Two.

List One is the start of finding the services and keywords for your location OutPosts. Chances are that your current HQ website is doing very well for your core services and keywords but does not penetrate every town, county or state nationally. So take that good work into geographic areas that you would like to be getting more work from, but are not currently.

When I started creating OutPosts for my marketing agency I set up small web development websites for large towns that were currently just out of our reach with our HQ website. Within a couple of months we were getting enquiries for decent sized projects within these towns, giving almost an infinite return on investment considering the small amount of time we put in.

List Two is where your niche marketing areas are. They are the areas in which you know there is potential as your accounts show you sell in those areas, but your main HQ site and mainstream marketing simply does not go far enough to attract enough business.

My agency always received a ton of website development and SEO work, but just could not crack the photography, video and audio services we were offering. So we spun out a sub-brand, Yomp VAP (video, audio, photography), created an OutPost **www.yompvap.com** which now receives many enquiries in its own right for this set of services that we were selling but just not receiving the enquiries for.

Keyword research

Every TrailBlazer OutPost you create will begin with keyword research. This is a fundamental component of the process, as the quality of your keywords and subsequent domain choices based on those keywords will dictate a large part of your success.

What you are doing is creating a micro-website around specific keywords; this is known as a 'pull' marketing strategy. You want people to find it online and therefore it must attract niche searches across a small number of keyword phrases.

I recommend starting with a geographic area and a specific service you offer. For example, if you are targeting a regional area outside your usual location and you are an accountant, go for something like 'Accountant Woking' as the main key phrase for the micro-site. The service descriptive phrase is 'accountant' and the geographic area is 'Woking'.

Most of an OutPost's evaluation criteria can be completed using a tool called Google AdWords Keyword Planner. This is an online resource that allows advertisers to search for keywords that they might be interested in pursuing for advertising. However, as Digital TrailBlazers we have reverse engineered it for keyword research (which it was never really intended for).

Take your list of services and keywords, add them into the planner and find out which ones have the most traffic within that area. They will become the focus for your OutPosts.

TRAILBLAZER MASTERY

Advanced TrailBlazer OutPosts has a 9 Step OutPost Keyword research system that will highlight which keywords to go after and which keywords to not waste time and money on. The system is very data and spreadsheet driven and therefore too detailed for this book. – Check out **www.digitaltrailblazer.co.uk/mastery** to access the system.

The next step is to select the most relevant keywords with a high number of monthly searches and make that your primary keyword. Buy the exact matching (if possible) URL for this keyword to start setting up your website. The exact match keyword for the URL helps you get up the search engines quicker when you are a micro website.

Now you have your URL – say it's **www.business coachhampshire.co.uk** (exact match from Business Coach Hampshire) – you need to create a micro-website. I would recommend asking a developer to knock it out for you quickly. Otherwise WordPress or other website development tools are great to use.

Create four to five pages around you and the service you are offering, all with unique content, plus add a blog or news feed so more content can easily be added. My recommendation is to brand it differently to your HQ website, as you could potentially find in time that both your OutPost and your HQ website are on the first page of Google for the same search term. Having two brands and two types of website makes you twice as likely to get enquiries. Most people get three quotations for services, so if you do this correctly you could be getting 66.6% of all the enquiries. If you are feeling confident and the keyword is important enough, set up a third micro-website and lock your competition out of page one.

For now, presume that you have chosen wisely and the geographic area is not covered by your HQ, so your website is set up as an individual coaching business in Hampshire (for example).

Place all three Trail-Trackers on the OutPost and a quality InfoSwap and you will have the basis for a lead generating machine. From this point you need to plan to update the website at the very least monthly, with more content and articles around the core keywords you are targeting. You will also need to complete a light search engine optimisation (SEO) campaign both internally and externally to the OutPost, to move up the rankings and hit that all important page one result within your niche.

Search engine optimisation will be covered later, so for now set up your first OutPost and then work through this book's SEO section for details on how to take it forward.

Once completed, you will have an asset that will pay out with leads over and over again and you will very quickly be building multiple OutPosts across multiple towns, cities and regions for many different niche services.

Asset #3 – Trail-Scouts

When out on the mountain ranges, especially in untravelled areas, the great explorers of yesteryear used Scouts as key members of the team.

They were the first people sent into an unexplored location to provide reconnaissance for the leadership team. They worked hard to obtain, distribute, and share vital geographical, directional, local information, including the local population's ability to help the expedition.

The Scout is a lone ranger and the eyes and ears of your team.

Digital TrailBlazers create Trail-Scouts

A Trail-Scout is an online page that someone can visit or land on and is designed *solely* for one single action from the website visitor.

The practical marketing purpose of this one-page website is for it to stand alone from your website, have traffic driven to it from a single marketing channel and perform one single objective. This method allows for total clarity of performance and results from that one single marketing channel.

By stand alone, I mean that it has no ties to your website, for example, no header links to other pages. It roams the untravelled areas of the internet alone, only accessible from the link you're providing in your marketing content (the call-to-action in an email, for example). So like the Scouts of the great Victorian explorers, our Trail-Scouts are lone rangers providing the eyes and ears of a single task.

There are two reasons why TrailBlazers use a Trail-Scout:

1. **Lead generation** – to entice visitors to leave you their details so you can contact them further in the future. They take a lead from an anonymous visitor to David Smith with his email and phone number.
2. **To warm up potential customers** (who you already have the details of) to the service or product you are trying to sell to them. This usually means that you are asking your database to self-select if they are interested in finding out more information and therefore become a warmer lead than just sitting in your database.

This creates the need for two types of Trail-Scout – a lead generation Scout and a warming up Scout. Let's look at an example campaign for each category:

Example Campaign using a Lead Generation Trail-Scout.

A property company with a new development to sell houses for lists the properties on its website, but wants to really drive sales for this new development, so decides that it will run multiple marketing campaigns for it.

They decide to use a Pay-Per-Click Advert campaign through Google AdWords to pay for website visitors who are looking to buy houses within that area. The company do not want to drive traffic to their main website because they do not want visitors getting distracted by all the other properties upon there. Plus they want to really maximise conversions from their website visitors and track exactly what their investment in Google AdWords brings them.

They create a Trail-Scout that is dedicated to the new development.

The content and pictures on the new Trail-Scout sells the dream of the new development, but holds back the property brochure and floorplans for interested people to use the InfoSwap download to access a copy.

The Trail-Scout also has a tracking telephone number on it and puts a thank you page behind the InfoSwap form so that it can track the number of conversions per month within Google analytics.

That's the three Trail-Trackers in place.

They then start the campaign through Google Adwords and they are able to see the following statistics from the campaign each month:

Website visitors from Pay-Per-Click
using Google AdWords = 550

Cost of website traffic = £687.50
(average cost per click was – £1.25)

Downloads of InfoSwap = 35

Tracking phone calls received = 17

Total Leads = 52

Cost per lead = £13.22

They run the campaign for a few months and find that they are converting one in ten leads into a sale, so the cost per sale = £132.20

Considering the property company makes on average £10,000 commission per sale of a house on the new development, they are absolutely delighted and as they have full clarity and transparency using the Trail-Scout and the Trail-Trackers. Using the data they then go on to keep on increasing the budget within the Pay-Per-Click campaign, making sure that the cost per lead remains around the £13 mark.

In fact, in the above example they may well decide that they are happy with the cost per lead increasing. As long as the 'lead to sale' close rate still stacks up and the campaign is profitable, then the sky's the limit.

Example Campaign using a 'Warming Up' Trail-Scout

A business consultant has a database of 1,000 contacts that she has gathered throughout the last three years since she quit her corporate job. Every now and then she sends them an email with a link to a new blog post she has written on leading teams or managing change within a business, but so far she has not seen any real response from her emails. So she decides that instead of giving away her thoughts and opinions freely, she will package up her next few blog posts and publish then as a small e-book. The e-book will be written to solve a specific problem, within a specific niche and will be targeted at the perfect audience for her related training programme that she would like to sell more of.

She creates an e-book entitled *Managing your first five staff as an entrepreneur*. She knows that most of her database are business owners, but she would like to work with ambitious entrepreneurs who are still small but want to grow. This e-book will help that database self-select if they fit her desired target market, simply by downloading a book with that title.

To make it as easy as possible for them, she created a Trail-Scout with a bit of content explaining the e-book, a few bullet points re-capping the benefits of reading it and a few testimonials from supportive test audience entrepreneurs who she had asked to read the e-book and comment.

She also created a thank you page with the e-book as a PDF so they can instantly access it, as well as a tracking telephone number for any direct questions or enquiries.

She then created an email and sent it to the database of 1,000 and the following results were:

Database size = 1,000

Email opens = 440

Email click through to Trail-Scout = 130

E-book downloads = 45

Tracking Phone Calls = 24

Total Leads = 69

She made appointments to see as many of the 69 leads as she could and was able to successfully fill her 30-person training course that started the following month.

From these two examples you can see how having a stand-alone page with a single purpose helps to either develop a new database or to warm up an existing one. A Trail-Scout is a very important part of your online armoury and should be used as much as possible.

Let's now look at the key elements you should include within the single page, if you are going to maximise the conversions on it.

Trail-Scouts - key considerations

When you send out your Trail-Scouts they need to have clear set goals and only one for each individual scout. When designing the page make sure you focus solely on what you want the visitor to do.

Make the title of the page the lead benefit of the InfoSwap, with perhaps a subtitle underneath with a fact to back up the lead benefit.

At the top of the page list all the benefits, usually in a simple bullet point list.

The page should have few images, but a well-designed relevant header graphic that entices the viewer into the desired action works well.

Add a badge, rosette or sticker graphic to the header image reaffirming the objective of the page. For example, 'Industry leading guide – Download Now'.

The position of the InfoSwap form (top right or centre) is externally important as this is the first place on a webpage that users naturally look.

Reaffirm the key benefits that the sign up form brings you with more bullet points above the form.

Place testimonials or awards you have received under the InfoSwap form, to show credibility

Make the page easy to scan and navigate.

TRAILBLAZER MASTERY

A/B test different versions of the Trail-Scout to make sure you have the most highly converting pages for your service. Some example variations could be shortened text, more bullets, different images, different colour schemes, different special offers or service bundles. Head over to **www.digitaltrailblazer.co.uk/mastery** to find out more.

So, remember a well-designed and deployed Trail-Scout is designed to close the deal; they create an environment where an ever increasing return on investment can be generated. A great Scout doesn't just produce better conversions; it can also save you money on your advertising costs.

For a list of links to example Trail-Scouts head over to **www.digital trailblazer.co.uk/trail-scout**

Your SummitTeam

When climbing your business growth mountain you need people around you that you can trust, hold accountable and rely upon.

The first successful Everest team brought four different skills to the mountain: they had the climbers, the support team, the press and a psychologist.

As a TrailBlazer you will be able to use the tools in this book to formulate your Trail-MAP and understand the Digital Assets required to start climbing your business growth mountain, but to make sure you really drive your business towards its targeted 12-month summit, you will need to evaluate your current team and also add additional members to make sure your achieve your goals.

Through working with hundreds of high achieving service sector businesses, my recommendation is that you split your team into five key skills sets:

SummitTeam = Fulfilment, Strategy, Marketing, Sales, and Support

This is an opportunity to review your internal and third-party teams that fulfil the orders your business receives. You need to look at the products and services you sell and make sure that they are not standing in the way of your growth. The most important part of being a Digital TrailBlazer is that your product works and it adds measurable value to your customers.

Fulfilment

Do not even leave your BaseCamp cabin if your fulfilment team are not up to the job. As the team carrying out the service you provide to your customers, set review parameters for them, training and performance linked bonuses if you can. Think about being the best of the best and get the team in place to do this.

Becoming a Digital TrailBlazer presumes you know how to do what you do, but never rest on your laurels, always strive for improvement, do not be afraid at this point to engage industry experience in specific fulfilment areas if you still do not feel you are adding the value you should to your customer base.

Strategy

I recommend that every business owner has a third party that they use to keep them on target and the straight and narrow. If you decided to bring in a coach or business consultant to do this, I recommend that they attend a dedicated monthly meeting to review targets. It is *so* important for you to be kept on target to achieve the growth you have planned for. A good adviser will be able to help you understand your team, yourself and your goals; they should also hold you and your team accountable for deliverables and hitting targets set.

Marketing

As becoming a digital TrailBlazer relies heavily on lead generation you need to look at who in your current marketing team (including yourself) has the skills required to climb your business growth mountain. Once you know your current in-house capacity and capability, then look to bring specialists in and out of the business on a retained or part-time capacity, to implement all the core TrailBlazer elements (HQ site, OutPosts, SEO, etc) needed to climb to your peak.

As a guide, your TrailBlazer Marketing Department could be made up of the following skills: Graphic Design, Web

Development, Animation/Video Production, Copywriting, Social Media Marketing, Google AdWords (Pay-per-Click) SEO and E-mail Marketing. I would not recommend as a small service based business taking on all these tasks in-house. You would have to overpay and train new staff members which will far out weigh the cost of using third-party specialists who do this all day every day for many businesses like yours.

If you are outsourcing a number of these elements I recommend appointing an internal Marketing Manager who does not have to be full-time and could be one of your fulfilment team with one day a week dedicated to managing your marketing. Their responsibility will be to focus upon taking your strategic decisions and keeping all parties on track, but also to make sure the ROI statistics are being generated and presented back to you so that you can make the big decisions on how and where to spend your budget.

Sales

You, or if you have a sales team *they*, need to be on the ball when becoming a Digital TrailBlazer. That said, a number of the activities you do online may well generate sales directly through developing small products or subscriptions that can be brought online.

In reality, for service sector businesses your main sales work involves either human communication via the phone, email, or face to face. For this reason you need to make sure that you use a solid Client Relationship Management system (CRM) and have individuals who are responsible for sales (if you are a small business this may be you). They must buy into your process and follow up the leads that the marketing team produce in double quick time.

The average website visitor who enquires about a service business's offering will give the company until the next morning at most to respond, without feeling a negative effect about that company. As Digital TrailBlazers we really want to be responding within the hour.

That is when the prospect is the hottest and they may be still in search mode, looking for alternative suppliers (your competition). If you can have preliminary telephone call with them while they are still looking for alternative quotes, you will be firstly breaking their concentration away from all others and secondly the first one to contact them and to perhaps get the most favourable sales presentation meeting time.

Having a sales team in place that understands and buys into this is a vital step forward. Never forget sales guys are brilliant when they are in their flow; keep them on target and keep on rewarding them and they will repay the favour. There is nothing worse than under-motivated, under-incentivised sales people.

Support

Like the great explorers of yesteryear we all need a good support team to feed us information about our climb. The most important of these is a good accountant who understands your goals and knows your Trail-MAP. You may even want to ask them to be involved in the production of each one annually and to join you at quarterly Check Point meetings, so they understand what you are trying to achieve and the numbers you need to produce to track progress.

For larger companies, having a good HR outsourcing company has paid dividends for businesses I have worked with. An HR company that helps you manage your staff appraisals and legal compliance and is also an impartial point of contact for your staff, is invaluable. As the business owner, getting bogged down in compliance is a nightmare. Leave it to the professionals where you can.

So there you are, your SummitTeam is in place, now you are ready to start your hike up the mountain and to leave the warm confines and security of your BaseCamp hut.

Take one last look around and make sure we have everything ready…

Final BaseCamp Preparation and Checklist:

We know exactly where we are going to –
12 Month Targets

We know how fast we are going to climb –
Monthly Forecasts

We have the right action plan to get there –
Your Trail-MAP

We know what and where our check points are –
The Digital TrailBlazer 5-step Process

We know what every team member's role is –
Your SummitTeam

We know how we are going to track progress –
Trail-Trackers

We know our key sales messages – Your USP's

We understand who we are targeting and why they will buy – Target Market

We know what we do well and why we are unique –
Your USPs

We know what we need to do in order to break even? –
Trail-MAP

Let's hit the Trail…

CHECK POINT 2 – DIGITAL TRAILBLAZERS SELL MORE TO EXISTING CLIENTS

'I have never worked a day in my life without selling. If I believe in something, I sell it, and I sell it hard.'
ESTÉE LAUDER

Did you know that you are sitting on a Gold Mine?

Prospective Digital TrailBlazers are usually shocked at how much value they find in their current and past customer database.

The easiest prospects to sell to, already buy from you!

On average it takes five to ten times more effort, time and cost to win new customers than it takes to sell to existing ones, and the average spend of a repeat customer is an enormous 67% more than a new one.

The aim of this section is to make selling 'easy' – easier to sell wider, deeper and further to your existing clients. I know it's mad, but most sales people sell once to a prospect then move on to the next. Who do you think picks up that customer's unfulfilled need the next time they are looking to buy?

Your competition does!

Remember, your customers know, like and trust you already. They truly are your lowest hanging fruit, so let's get picking!

The TrailBlazer Divide and Conquer Matrix

The divide and conquer matrix is all about looking at your current customer base and communicating the correct messages to the appropriate customers. There is nothing worse than receiving marketing communications from a company about a service they offer that you already use. It shows that they do not know you as a customer, you are not important enough to be given special 'customer only' messages and that the company is seriously poor at keeping data on their own clients.

As a TrailBlazer you need to be smarter than the average business that continues to spam their own clients!

The matrix we use is simple:

Take a spreadsheet and list all your clients down the left-hand side, it is ok to have hundreds, it will make this activity even more rewarding when it is done.

Along the top of the spreadsheet list all the products you sell to your customers. Add everything even if it is a small side product.

Go down the client list and tick each service that that the client has bought from you. The many blank spaces left shows where the value is within your current client base.

You simply take each service and tell the clients who have not yet brought it why they should, and populate the matrix with more ticks as you successfully convert each client.

EXERCISE

Go to TrailBlazer Mastery tool kit **www.digitaltrailblazer.co.uk /mastery** and download the TrailBlazer Divide and Conquer Matrix and unlock the massive value you are sitting upon, for yourself.

Productisation and sub-branding of your services

Digital TrailBlazers who productise their services give themselves a distinct competitive advantage over their competition.

Productisation is the act of turning a successful service into a commercial product. It is the Holy Grail for Digital TrailBlazers because it allows us to package repetitive processes, achieve scale, increase profitability and drive new growth from our existing as well as new client bases. It also shows us where new products can be created and up-sold or cross-sold to the existing client base to increase their annual spend with you.

Services are tough to appraise, but products are easy

Existing or potential clients looking to work with a company on a new project will usually perform what's known as a 'Beauty Parade'. This is where a company will bring three to five firms in to pitch for the work, slowly reducing down to two or three companies, which they will play off against each other to get the best deal.

The power is firmly in the client's hands.

As Digital TrailBlazers, we want to market and pitch our services so they stand head and shoulders above the competition. We also want the new products to be easily assessed for their virtues against the client's 'problem' not against other competitors. Creating products like this is what keeps your customers locked into your services and prevents a beauty parade each time your clients require a new service or one of your projects finishes.

The art is to make customers feel happy entering into one of your packaged services which in an ideal world has a monthly retained element to keep the customer buying from you.

As an example, if you are looking to buy wireless headphones for the first time it is easy to evaluate their merits: you listen to the sound quality, see if the integration with your smart phone is easy, check out the features and decide on whether or not it is the right shape, size, colour or weight.

However, you cannot so easily evaluate accounting, marketing, consulting, logistics or any other service sector business the same way. Instead, prospective clients let you pitch in person, look for examples of your past work, ask for client references, check your online presence/reviews and attempt to evaluate the various components of your proposed solution.

As Digital TrailBlazers we want to rise above this, easing the buying apprehensions of our potential and current clients by making our services more tangible, unique and outstanding than our competition.

Key considerations when you are creating your productised service

Start by listing all the features the service has, with clear benefits to the client of each feature.

List the expected deliverables for the service: what does the client get during and at the end of the service?

Give the new product a name, so it effectively becomes a sub-brand that ties in with your main brand but has its own identity.

A physical brochure or a rate card (price list) for the productised service makes it more tangible and will also become an integral part of your new pitch.

Having set packages and prices will help with the selling process; this rules out lengthy proposal stages which are opportunities for you to be forgotten, plus time consuming for you.

Identifying the names of people who will do the work adds credibility. They become part of the brand and people do buy people, so this will help to firm up your relationships and add to your productised service.

With these in mind, list your current services and see if you can productise them. Think about presenting them as, for instance, Gold, Silver and Bronze level packages.

Once you have done this, think about how you can now present to your current customers the same services they already know you offer, but in this new productised look. Use the Divide and Conquer Matrix to find out who has not brought this service yet and try them out with the newly productised version of the service.

Done properly this should get you some quick and easy sales from your existing customer base.

10 Ways to sell more to Existing Customers

Now that you are ready to increase your revenue per customer, here are some tried and tested Digital TrailBlazer methods for getting your sales staff focused on up-selling, cross-selling and marketing additional services.

1. Tailored customer email marketing

Most businesses looking to become a Digital TrailBlazer will already have a customer base. Some may only have a small pool of customers, others will have hundreds if not thousands, but how often do you send them special communications to reflect their special status?

Not often enough?

One of the most effective strategies to sell more to existing customers is to make them feel special and talk to them regularly as customers. If a client of yours is reminded of how great you are through a special email communication each month that is tailored specifically for them, their loyalty to and identity as your client will grow. You can then drop in special offers for new products or services or exclusive invites to customer only events.

This method could well be more important than your blanket marketing emails to your non-customer database and more fruitful in terms of sales. Use the Divide and Conquer Matrix to find out who to market to first.

2. Customer only networking events

One way to win multiple times over is to organise events just for your customers. Not only will these events give you the opportunity to see all your clients in one go, which clearly will optimise you and your team's time, but it will also allow them to meet each other.

These events will give your customers their own opportunity to find new customers, suppliers and partnerships from the attendees in an informal networking fashion. To help this, before the event think about who each customer would most benefit from meeting. You can even introduce them at the event and take further credit helping them grow their business.

Yomp Marketing's accountant Kass Verjee from the Financial Management Centre does this expertly. He hosts afternoon BBQs or evening supper clubs on a Saturday for his clients at the fabulous, grand Oatlands Park Hotel in Weybridge. I attend almost every one because I always meet new clients and suppliers at the events. Of course there are always a few of Kass' potential clients there who are just in the process of deciding whether to become a client of his. If I meet one of his prospects I of course sing his praises to them, for which he is always grateful for, but will never ask me to do so. He simply sets up the environment for this to happen, introduces people in his charming way and let's the magic happen.

A very sharp operator.

So back to your client event...

Once you have a busy room full of clients, introduce an interesting speaker to present to them, or entertainment that you know they would enjoy as a focal point. Before and after this focus point, put yourself in front of everyone, thank them for coming and perhaps drop in some important news or the launch of a new product you think they would find useful.

Maybe bring a few clients on stage who have tested the new product for social proof, so clients feel that this would work for them if it has worked well for the test clients. Don't over-sell it and allow for more information to be delivered in one-to-one conversations or by meeting with each individual client after the event to show that you respect them as individuals. But always have a way people can sign up on the day, because remember the attendees already buy from you so why not buy a little more there and then?

3. Ask for referrals and build a loyalty programme

Your customers, your business contacts and the people who you regularly network with already 'know, like and trust you'. The entrepreneur behind 4Networking, the largest joined-up UK Business Networking Company, Brad Burton, has built his business which hold 5,000+ events per year, from this mantra.

Your customers are already using your services, they know what you do for them and they like it. So who better to ask to refer you to other similar businesses who you can help?

Better still, we all know that a handful of clients will become brand advocates for you: they will sing your praises whenever they are given an opportunity to do so.

But are you missing out on opportunities your contacts could put your way, such as the other clients and close contacts, or even your suppliers?

A well-thought out loyalty programme will help grow your business.

When we launched our loyalty programme at Yomp we were really surprised at the uptake and after a few months we were already paying thousands of pounds of commission to multiple partners to thank them for an introduction to other companies who use our services.

One of our partners, Peter Dixon, said the clearly laid out commission structure and the well-executed launch event meant referrals just came naturally because he had Yomp in mind each time he met new clients or networked with new businesses. Of course he would always pitch his coaching business, but when marketing came into the conversation it became easy to drop in Yomp's name and follow up with an email introduction to Yomp for the customer. 'The rest was down to Yomp' he added.

EXERCISE

For inspiration upon how you may set up your referral structure, why not check out our HQ Site section and collateral we use on the Yomp Partner Program Page – **www.yompmarketing.com/partner-program**

4. Special offers through direct and email marketing

We all know that talking to your customers is important but we need to give value when we communicate with them. This could be in terms of advice, but every now and then why not offer your loyal clients a special offer just for them?

Contacting them by email marketing and direct mail with a special offer will surprise you with the response. Your customers sometimes know about a service of yours they need, they may even have mentioned it to you, but had not quite made the decision to buy; or you may not have any idea that they do want it. A well-timed email or letter may give them the nudge they need to push this forward.

When constructing a special offer, don't be embarrassed by the fact it is a discount on a service: think about what you can add to a service in a bundle then discount it when put together; or what would make the customer excited about a particular new product that you could give as an introductory offer. In my experience, a blanket 15% off all products and services never has the same reaction because it is untargeted and unspecific.

Always make sure it has a start and end date for urgency and a clear call to action, perhaps back to an 'especially for my clients' Trail-Scout that will then convert them better.

5. Give referrals back to your customers and track

This is a great strategy and has to be done with a little finesse. We all know how great it is when we receive a hot lead from someone we know, better still they have talked to the potential new customer before introducing you and sold you and your product before you even knew that this potential client existed.

It is a great feeling walking into a sales meeting when the hard work is done and all you need to do is beam with personality and get them to sign on the dotted line. You come away from that new sale feeling indebted to the introducer and you of course want to help them as much as you can. If they are your supplier you may even buy more from them because of it.

So if we love that happening to us, then why not give more referrals to our customers as a way of getting them to buy more from us? It will certainly strengthen your relationship with them and even if they do not make the sale, you have shown them you are thinking of them as more than just a customer.

The best way Yomp have found to make this happen is to incorporate it into our Partner Programme. As part of this programme we offer commissions for any closed business referral given to us but we do not ask for anything back the other way, we simply just track in our monthly reports the businesses we have introduced to them. We then make sure they receive this document monthly to help them track the referrals we have given to them. Ideally they will give us feedback about which leads the business has converted and which are pending (so we give our contact a little nudge and get the deal over the line), and those which were not good referrals, so we can learn to refer better.

This method has been great for Yomp and I guarantee will help grow the average spend from each of your customers.

If your customer's business is booming, then yours will too.

6. Customer catch-up appointment setting

Stay in touch. Sometimes you may not naturally see your best customers as often as you'd like, so you need to work extra hard to keep yourself on their radar screens. Your campaigns may be going really well, but you need to make sure your client feels loved and appreciated. There is nothing better for this than some one-on-one / company-to-company time.

Work out the most important person to be in the meeting – sometimes this might not be the business owner but the one person who you may worry is not fully on board with your project, or who you feel is the key decision maker – then create a catch-up meeting so you can get feedback from the work completed to date and also go back over the strategy for the future. Of course, make sure that that strategy has an element of an up-sell product or complementary cross-sell. Then book the meeting. In the connected world, a Skype or Google Hangout format could work just as well for international or distance clients, but if you can go and see them, do so.

One tactic that Digital TrailBlazers have found works well is to create a spreadsheet with all their customers on it, with the dates that they have gone to see them. This will give you a picture of who is being seen the most and who is being a little neglected, and can then create powerful comparisons with time into each client vs income out of each client. Are you spending too much time on unprofitable clients? Are you not spending enough time on important clients? – Remember the 80/20 rule: 80% of your turnover will usually come from 20% of your customer base, so just make sure your focus is in the correct places.

7. Customer-only website login areas

To help make your customers feel special, why not think of creating an online community and login area for them upon your website? Having a place where they can login and easily communicate with each other will allow them to ask questions and either have them answered by you or in some busy online communities clients answer questions for other clients and share the experiences they have had along the way.

It does not always have to be on your website. Daniel Priestley, who wrote *Key Person of Influence* has a private Facebook group for entrepreneurs who go onto complete his premium training course. The benefit of the Facebook group is that it pops up in your news feed when you are not necessarily looking for it and creates an easy to access community for his customers. LinkedIn can also be used effectively in the same way.

You can also put together login areas where your customers can download free resources: this again will help clients to engage with your content and in some instances be introduced to new ideas, therefore making it easy to sell more to them at a later date. With all these tactics, make sure you are giving value first and selling second. Your customers do not want to feel bombarded with sales messages without getting value back first.

8. No-brainer up-sells and cross-sells

To be honest, this should be number one on the list, but I wanted to warm you up first before we went back to the easiest and quickest method!

When you get them right, no-brainer up-sells can be so fruitful and easy; they do not need to be hard to sell or add £100s per month onto the clients' bills. At Yomp we offer tracking telephone numbers for under £10 a month for each marketing campaign we conduct for our clients: this gives us the valuable inbound call data that is a no-brainer to add to the campaign cost at such a low cost. We also offer hosting for the websites we build: we are neither the cheapest nor the most expensive, but priced in a way that makes it a no-brainer for clients to use us for their hosting as it keeps it all under one roof. These up-sells produce significant income for Yomp and help our clients feel comfortable that their requirements are being looked after by a supplier they trust.

It's a win/win

Another example is Scott Gerber, founder of SizzleIt, a New York City company that produces short promotional videos.

'We started noticing that our clients wanted us to store their media files because they had a habit of re-editing their video reels several times over the course of the year.'

This process became time-consuming, data storage-consuming and tedious for the company, so Gerber started charging clients monthly to store their data.

'This created a whole new revenue stream for the company, not to mention it allowed us to get rid of large amounts of media files when clients didn't want to pay.'

This was a no-brainer for clients who wanted to work on a number of projects and because storage is not expensive, clients feel comfortable that their data is being looked after and managed.

EXERCISE

List your top 20% of your customer base, then ask yourself "what no-brainer products are most common across all of them?" When you have the list pick the top 2 or 3 and productise them properly and add them to every new proposal that goes out. This in its self will generate a considerable uplift in turnover from your current customer base.

9. Ask for feedback, listen and create new products/services

Why not give customers a say in what you sell?

After all, they know the problems they are having in their business just as well as you know your market – maybe even better.

An example for Digital TrailBlazers is fashion house ModCloth who started an initiative called 'Be the Buyer'. This campaign engaged with their client base and asked them to vote online from a selection of clothing samples.

If a sample got enough votes, they added it to their e-commerce store. To back this up they sent emails to visitors who voted for the item congratulating them on their choice and of course offering the garment up for sale. They then used this 'social proof' to email the rest of their customer base and say that this particular item was selected by customers 'just like you', demonstrating that they listen to and understand their client base.

Programs like this allow Digital TrailBlazers to confidently create and promote products that might have not been thought of or considered too risky previously. It also encourages a high level of customer engagement which of course leads to repeat sales. This level of openness and engagement, even for service-based businesses, can help mould and develop your offering and grow the average customer spend per year.

10. Tiered pricing structures

Your business may be facing a pricing crisis and you don't even know it...

Building a business around a single price per product is like standing on one leg: you can do it for a while, but in the long run you will fall down. For one thing, single price product companies are vulnerable to a competitor capable of building a better (and maybe cheaper) version of your product. That's why many companies begin with one product but quickly evolve into a multi-product business with a tiered pricing model. Doing this allows you to not only appeal to a wider base of potential customers, but it also makes it easier to communicate the value of specific features and functionality.

Of course, the task of creating and pricing multiple variations of the one product isn't always simple. To do it, you will need to answer two key questions:

Which features belong in which variation?

How should each variation be priced?

Those might seem like simple questions to answer, but doing so actually requires a framework that ensures no tier is too heavy (or light) on features, and that the value of upgrading is clear and compelling.

From working with our Digital TrailBlazers we have come up with four steps for developing a tiered pricing structure:

1. Look at your overall service and determine the frequency of use and value delivered of each individual feature that makes up the service. This will identify which features should go with which version. Also, consider offering some options as add-on features with narrow appeal but high value.
2. Evaluate functional differences from your customer's perspective between versions in terms of value and price relative to each other.
3. Balance your entry-level price with the prices of your higher value editions, do not create massive leaps in value or cost.
4. Test and get feedback from as many customers as possible by asking them if they would recognise these tiers and whether they are valuable enough for them to consider upgrading to.

The basic goal of this process is to take a closer look at the value differences between versions so it makes sense to you and the customer. While you want to make sure that customers are paying for the functional value they receive, it's also important not to make the price steps between editions so high that the buyers won't upgrade because they don't think they're getting a reasonable deal.

Here's where a certain degree of strategy is involved in developing and deploying a multi-edition, tiered pricing model:

If your company's goal is to attract as many new customers as possible, you might choose a low entry price. That being said, while a low entry price with small price steps between editions may encourage upgrades, it could also limit the price you can charge for your premium editions.

If you want to be paid fairly for premium editions and want the price steps to be reasonable, you'll need to consider a higher entry-level price. The problem with that approach? Higher prices typically lower the attractiveness of the entry-level product and limit the number of new customers.

The conflict between low entry price and premium edition prices arises because buyers look at the price and value of each product edition relative to each other to decide which edition is right for them. So, you have to ask yourself: is the entry price low enough to encourage purchase? And does the price and added functionality from edition to edition encourage or discourage upgrades?

However, get this system correct and you will soon see your current customers moving up from tier to tier, spending more per year with you than you would have thought previously possible on a one-price product strategy.

CHECK POINT 3 – DIGITAL TRAILBLAZERS FIND NEW CLIENTS

'Many a small thing has been made large by the right kind of advertising.'

MARK TWAIN

HILLARY AND NORGAY GO UP EVEREST
Edmund Hillary and Tenzing Norgay were part of the British 1953
Everest Expedition, led by Colonel John Hunt.

Hunt had selected a team of people who were experienced climbers from all around the British Empire. Among the 11 chosen climbers, Edmund Hillary was selected as a climber from New Zealand and Tenzing Norgay, though born a Sherpa, was recruited from his home in India. Also along for the trip was a filmmaker to document their progress and a writer for *The Times*, both there in the hopes of documenting a successful climb to the summit. Very importantly, a physiologist rounded out the team.

After months of planning and organising, the expedition began to climb. On their way up, the team established nine camps, some of which are still used by climbers today.

Out of all the climbers on the expedition, only four would get a chance to make an attempt to reach the summit. Hunt, the team leader, selected two teams of climbers. The first team consisted of Tom Bourdillon and Charles Evans; the second team consisted of Edmund Hillary and Tenzing Norgay.

The first team left on May 26, 1953 to reach the summit of Mount Everest. Although the two men made it up to about 300 feet shy of the summit, the highest any human had yet reached, they were forced to turn back after bad weather set in as well as a fall and problems with their oxygen tanks.

As Digital TrailBlazers going up our business growth mountains we know that the concentrated planning in BaseCamp and the quick and easy to unlock value from our current customer base has helped us to get this far upon our mountain. We may well be already achieving dizzy new heights, but this is not time to rest on our achievements to date, if we are not to fall short fall short like Bourdillon and Evans then we have to push on and grow our customer base.

By now we can demonstrate our USPs and we know why our current customers brought from us in the first place. We also have systems and tactics in place to make sure they continue to buy from us. So now it is time to spread the word.

From interviews I have conducted with many small service sector business owners, their number one biggest struggle is finding good quality clients.

Many businesses try to stay safe and stick to the few things that have worked well in the past. However, the key is to diversify your marketing channels, so if one channel dries up, there are a number of others still feeding leads into the business.

Keep in mind that what works for you now, might not work in six months' time.

A lot of the marketing channels for finding new clients are also great places to find mentors, partners, and suppliers, so keep an open mind.

The Digital TrailBlazer Stretch Further Technique

'Being everywhere is so important
in today's online world.'
CHRIS DUCKER

As the owner of a service sector business, you will have dabbled in a number of online channels. You may already have an HQ website with a blog or a news feed on which you put content periodically. You may also already have a personal Facebook account and you might have a company Twitter account, but have you really stretched your brand across all the important places online?

As Digital TrailBlazers, there are things we can do to reach more potential customers. Far more than if we were to just stick with writing content on our HQ websites through news articles or blog posts.

Putting content on your HQ website is just the start; gone are the days of bloggers having one website that people went back to time and time again. In today's online economy you have to engage with your audience everywhere they are and then draw them back to your HQ website or even to your OutPosts and Scouts so you can convert them from an anonymous member of your target audience into a real person whom you can help, entertain and ultimately make into a customer.

Getting far more eyes on your brand is vitally important and there is no better way to do this than with the idea of stretching further online.

There are two things that come with stretching further:

The first is reaching out on platforms beyond your HQ website to touch new audiences and attract new eyes to your brand. Eyes that would have never found you otherwise and are therefore potential new customers outside your current reach of influence. Online there are vast quantities of people who are hungry to devour your content, but they are never going to know about you if you are only focusing upon your HQ website.

Secondary, for the people who already know you, they will be far more committed to you and become even bigger fans of your brand, because you are not just a blogger anymore, you are a multimedia machine.

The result of this is that when anyone asks these contacts, 'Who do I go for information about your service (whatever it is)?', they're going to tell them to go to you, because you just seem to be everywhere online talking about your particular area of expertise.

Pat Flynn is an online training blogger, who has had 1.32 million unique visitors to his HQ website to date. To develop further, he wanted to find out how his audience found him first and therefore went to his audience and asked them one simple question:

'How did you find me?'

The results were incredible! He commented that:

> "Over 1,700 people responded in just two weeks. What are the top three ways that people who read my blog found me? Not Google, not Twitter, not Facebook, but number one is iTunes: 19% of people who now read my blog found my podcast on iTunes; 16% found me on YouTube; and 15% found me from a link from another website.
>
> Altogether, 50% of the people who now read my blog found me on iTunes, YouTube or links from other blogs. That number just blew my mind when I did this survey."

Results like this show that you should never underestimate which places online are important and which are not. If you stretch your brand online you will get more eyes on your content and convert more audience members into customers.

How to stretch further?

The first thing to note is – If your audience is not on there, then you should not be on there.

A target audience member for an accountancy business will not be on social networks aimed at young people, such as Snapchat, so do not spend time and investment in the wrong places – but keep monitoring these channels as the same would have been said for Facebook a few years ago.

As users grow up on social networks, the networks themselves start to mature with their audience; now Facebook is a lead generation machine for accountancy businesses, who can easily target business owners with adverts suited to them and generate substantial new business from the platform.

So make a list of all the places you know your target audience is online. Why not contact a few of them and ask them where they are currently engaging with content online, which blogs do they read, what social networks are they active on, which online forums do they use?

Once you have the list, check out the sites where you are not yet active, set up the accounts and make sure you get your brand consistent across all profiles. Try to use the same profile picture for you as the entrepreneur, and for company accounts make sure your logo and header images are consistent and eye-catching.

Do not overlook other blogs out there. For example, if you are a dog walking service, think about getting active on a magazine's website such as *Dogs Today*, ask to guest post with an article on their website, leave comments on their blogs with your name and a link back to your website within the post. Maybe even look to sponsor an event they are running or pay for advertising space on their website or in their magazine. If your target audience is reading articles on a third-party website, network or forum, get your brand on there too.

Once you are set up on these social networks, forums and websites, think about the one action that you would like your audience to take once they have seen your content and liked what you are saying.

As TrailBlazers, you should be trying to get them from an anonymous member of your target audience and into your sales funnel, getting them to click through to your HQ website or Trail-Scout so that you can convert them further into your database via an InfoSwap.

To do this really effectively, create specific pages upon your HQ website designed just for your Twitter followers, for example, or even create a Trail-Scout just for YouTube subscribers so they can get unique content from you, such as a private video training series, as a reward for them being part of your YouTube community. This method works really well and attracts a far higher percentage conversion rate of new audience members than just sending them to your HQ website home page.

Once you have your conversion strategy set up for the new places, start regularly sharing your content on them. If you write a blog on your HQ website, use all the new platforms to tell the world. Content should be cross-shared and conversations about it can be had on all the different places. Share your new videos on YouTube, but also tell your Facebook fans that it is there, and post a link to the video on your Facebook page as well. Sharing all your hard work is vitally important and dedicating as little as 20 minutes a day to doing so will have a dramatic effect on your audience and your conversions.

In Check Point #3 I will discuss how you turn up your volume across all these platforms, but first you need to get to the party before you can be the life and soul of it. So focus upon getting your brand out there, link back to your HQ, OutPost or Scouts and start engaging with your readers.

Customer Conversion Funnel

> It's impossible to map out a route to your
> destination if you don't know where
> you're starting from.
> **SUZE ORMAN**

To get to the top of Everest, Hillary and Norgay had the help of a big team. To hit your business growth mountain summit you also will need plenty of help.

In particular you will need plenty of customers.

To achieve this you will need to map out how they will join you. As TrailBlazers we do this through the Customer Conversion Funnel.

On the next page is an all-encompassing funnel for a service-based company.

It is an intricate list of stages, but do not be put off as some stages can be as short as a few questions. Having this in place allows the Marketing Team and Sales Team to understand the processes and make the transfer between departments as seamless as possible.

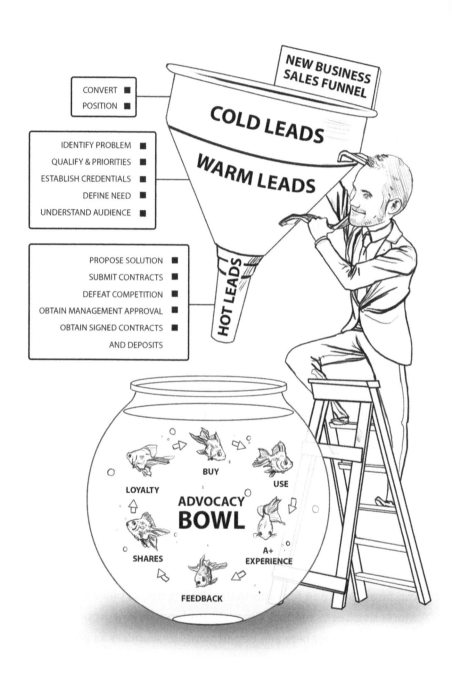

The start of the customer conversion funnel

The funnel is the process to which we take our converted lead and make them into a paying customer. Using your digital assets such as your HQ website, OutPost and Scouts, as well as engaging with your audience using the Stretch Further technique and some of the 10 ways to find new customers methods at the end of this Check-Point, you will find that an Anonymous Audience Member has been converted into a Lead and has been placed at the top of the funnel as Cold.

This is where the journey to become a customer starts.

Cold Leads

The funnel start off with all leads as cold until we are able to take them through the following four steps:

Convert an anonymous target audience members into a **Lead:** an individual or business who has given you their contact details, usually through your digital assets via InfoSwaps.

Position your service to the Lead by outlining common problems that you know the Lead and others like him / her have, and that you can solve.

Identify Problem – Follow up the Lead to confirm the problem exists.

Qualify and Prioritise – Before the first meeting make sure that the Lead meets the target audience segmentation profile that you have put together. Are they really in your target turnover group? Are they really able to pay your fees? Will they be more work than they are worth? Are they concerned enough about the problem?

Warm Leads

Establish Credentials – Book a meeting either face-to-face or via a video call. Present your company, promote your USPs, then use open questions to establish the Lead's specific Need.

Define Need – Recap to the client: What the Problem is, How you solve it, What is the expected return on investment (ROI's).

Understand Your Audience – Who are the decision makers (the people who ultimately will either give you the thumbs up or the thumbs down). Also find out who is most likely to be your Sponsor– (the person who likes you the most, probably the person who filled in the InfoSwap). Finally, who needs the most warming up? There is always someone who does not want to spend the money, or is the sponsor of one of your competing bids. Give them some extra love if you can.

Hot Leads

Propose Solution – Use a well-designed, well-written template proposal structure (brand consistency), with tailored sections around their Problem and your Solution. – Propose a Pilot (less of a commitment), if necessary.

Submit Contracts – Attached to the proposal, submit draft contracts for their legal team to look at. Allow for the pilot within the contract, so signatures are obtained before the pilot begins

Defeat Competition – Have individual discussions with each decision-maker, put most focus on least warm decision-makers and competitor sponsors. Find out where you are strong against them but also look at dispelling any perceived weaknesses of your service or your terms.

Obtain Management Approval – Make sure each management level has met their respective person in your business and all are happy to proceed. For example, ask one of your functional people to meet one-on-one with the equivalent in their business. Very few businesses go this extra mile and it can easily be the difference between the thumbs up and the thumbs down.

Obtain Signed Contracts and Deposits – Make sure that their financial and legal teams understand the financial and contractual requirements of your services.

Sales Conversion

Proof of Concept – Make sure you nail the pilot that allows the client to see value before committing long-term.

Deliver – Implement your service to the highest possible standards and keep regular communication going.

The Advocacy Bowl

The Advocacy stage is where you work with the newly converted customers and grow them into fans, then active advocates of your brand.

A brand advocate means a person or customer who feels delighted about a brand, product or service received, then passes on positive word-of-mouth messages about the brand to other people.

The exciting part of creating a working Advocacy Bowl is that your most loyal consumers are typically so satisfied with your products and services that they are motivated to talk about you and promote your business through word-of-mouth marketing.

These days, that word-of-mouth marketing presents an incredible opportunity as more and more conversations happen online, giving the kind words they are saying about you global exposure.

Understanding the importance of creating brand advocates for new business sales is half the job. Making everyone in your business aligned with this and performing in a way that delights your customers is the hardest task.

Author, speaker and acclaimed authority on sales Zig Ziglar comments:

> I have always said that everyone is in sales.
> Maybe you don't hold the title of salesperson, but
> if the business you are in requires you to deal with
> people, you, my friend, are in sales.

This is so true, as it only takes one bad experience of one of your members of staff for a customer who you have worked so hard to get on board to become disgruntled and worse still share their opinions with others which, if done online, can work against your marketing effects in a massive way.

To harness this powerful tool for finding new customers, we follow the stages below:

Advocacy Bowl Stages

Buy – This is where the Customer Conversion Funnel meets the Advocacy Bowl: now it is time to keep them so happy they never need to go into a funnel again.

Use – Get underway and make sure you do everything you promised.

A+ experience – Under-promise in the Proposal stage and over-deliver in the Use stage, making sure you build relationships with your customers all the way through the staff and management tiers. Everyone needs to be delighted with you, your staff and the end result you are giving.

Feedback – Work on 'How else can we help you?' optimisation. Regularly ask them what they are benefiting from? Can we help in other areas? What do they enjoy the most? What could we improve to make them even more delighted? – Cementing these questions into your process, (perhaps at every quarterly meeting for example), will give amazing feedback and ways to make an even better experience for your customer, but it will also keep on reminding them why they love working with you and will help to convert them into a proactive advocate

Shares – This is where you are now getting the benefit of their advocacy. They share why they love you with friends, contacts and also online. You are then able to take people who are referred to you by the advocate and put them into the top of your Customer Conversion Funnel, and the process starts for the new lead from cold all the way through until you have yet another customer and another potential new brand advocate.

Loyalty – As a result of putting their name to your service when recommending you to their friends. As well as having an A+ experience, the Advocate becomes more and more loyal and therefore…

Keeps on buying – An Advocate well looked after will not need to be sold to again, they will simply bond with your brand, staff, service or product and will not think twice about telling others about it. This is where your business gains massive value and following.

This CheckPoint is all about stretching your brand and message to all the places your target audience is engaging on the internet. Once there, converting the anonymous audience members to leads, then leads into customers, customers to brand advocates, then TrailBlazers find ways of generating new leads from the advocates, who in turn become new customers. It is a never ending circle, which if completed properly can rapidly grow your business.

Now we have a system, let's look at the first 10 things I would recommend you work on to supersize this process:

The 10 Most Effective Ways to Find New Customers

Relying on too few customers can leave you vulnerable: losing just one could mean you hit cash flow problems, staffing issues and suppliers' problems.

Even if it seems unlikely that you will lose customers, finding new people to sell to might be the best way to keep your business growing and heading to its 12-month summit.

Here are the 10 best ways you can win new customers without breaking the bank:

1. Sending out your Scouts

As discussed at BaseCamp, you Trail-Scouts are a web page that someone can visit or land on and are designed *solely* for one single action from the website visitor.

The practical marketing purpose of this *one-page website* is for it to stand alone from your website, have traffic driven to it from a single marketing channel and perform one single objective.

I love using Trail-Scouts for finding new customers, and I would like you to start setting them up everywhere you want to squeeze a customer into taking one single action.

For all the clients I have ever worked with, Trail-Scouts have become a fundamental part of their marketing and in my opinion should be used by every business, regardless of industry.

To help you send out your first wave of Trail-Scouts, here are a few ways you can use them:

- As the destination for every advert, be it pay-per-click (PPC) or offline (such as magazines), to lead people to a place to get more info
- To drive people to your events booking form
- To buy your book
- To subscribe your audience to your email newsletter
- As your social media profile links
- To promote your new Gold, Silver, Bronze productised service launch
- As a personalised destination in the 'About the Author' box from a guest blog post
- As a destination from a newspaper article written about you or your company
- To promote and download your free e-book
- As a destination for Facebook updates

When you are sending out your Trail-Scouts to find new customers, make sure you send the potential audience to a relevant and targeted page. Your HQ website's homepage is a mish-mash of goal-oriented communication, so resist the urge to send people there as it is better suited to the curious web-surfer than the person clicking through from a banner or AdWords link.

Think one goal, one message, one action. Hence one page – a Trail-Scout.

2. Establishing your OutPosts

Again from BaseCamp, we have the brilliant process to find gaps in your market and go after them using OutPosts, which are micro-websites focused around small niches or locations.

Business exposure is crucial nowadays and I see so many businesses cram vast quantities of information onto their websites with the intention of exposing all their products, services and locations to their customers.

They also want to be optimised and listed for all their services in all the geographic areas they operate within on Google and other search engines. But, since their website is so full of different information and services, it is hard for them to become specialised in a specific service or product. This results in a low page rank and not appearing on the first page for their product keyword searches.

To get started with establishing your OutPosts, here are the top five ways they can help you find new customers:

Keyword-focused OutPosts – If you offer six services and all are extremely competitive, you can create keyword-specific OutPosts for each service. This will get you a much quicker search engine rank than your HQ website, which will be trying to rank for six different services keywords.

Town- or county-focused OutPosts – You can buy a URL such as 'Builders Sussex' and create an OutPost for it, even if you are based in Kent. This will give you access to new customers you would have not previously touched.

Internationally-focused OutPosts – you can change all the images and the URL to a different country. For example, to target the Irish market a UK business might create an OutPost within its niche that is designed with an Irish brand and focus.

Language-based OutPosts – If your service crosses language barriers, you may find that your HQ website does not cross language listings. You may have a language converter on your HQ website, but to rank on foreign language search engines is another task in itself.

New Venture OutPosts – You may want to create a new sub-brand or set of complementary services, but not reference them on your HQ website. With an OutPost they can be branded differently, rank on the search engine for the relevant keywords and you can push test audiences through them to work out if the new venture is going to be a success before spending cash on them.

Thousands of internet savvy businesses have been implementing OutPosts in their online business model. Try typing in a city-based keyword, check Google local listings, and see how many websites are the same company. This gives companies more exposure, better SEO results and a competitive advantage – definitely worth using for your business.

3. **Optimising existing channels for conversion using A/B testing**

Increasing the new customers your business takes on can be as easy as reviewing what you are currently doing, tracking performance and then optimising each channel to get higher quality customers more quickly.

Testing should be at the core of all your marketing. Not only does it help you understand the impact you're making, but it gives you a much fuller understanding of your customers' behaviour and preferences. It not only tells you where you've been, but where you should (and shouldn't) go with your campaigns.

A/B testing is the simplest, most straightforward testing method available: an A/B test is a process through which you provide different versions of a piece of marketing. Send the same segments of the same audience through each different piece of marketing, track results and then go forward with the winning variation of the marketing.

If you are sending out email marketing you can A/B test email titles. To do this you can send one title to 10% of your database and a second title to another 10%. Make sure you keep everything else the same. Whichever title gets the best response rate is the one you send to the remaining 80% of the database to optimise your responses.

You can A/B test different newspaper adverts. Choose the same publication but across different weeks (one advert per week) you can test whether a black and white advert is better than a colour one, or if a half-page is better than a quarter-page advert. Alternatively you can keep the advert size the same and test advert headlines, or special offers

You can test different Trail-Scout designs for your pay-per-click campaigns. Google AdWords is great for having the same campaigns alternating the visitor click-throughs between two different Trail-Scouts. This will allow you to optimise the pages for the best covering offers or downloads.

Ideally, you should be consistently performing A/B testing across your entire marketing platforms. Each campaign can yield insights from an A/B test that can provide incremental lifts in responses that build on each other to optimise your lead generation.

To set up your A/B tests, cast your mind back to the Trail-Trackers section in BaseCamp and make sure all, or at least some, response tracking methods are on the marketing channel you would like to A/B test.

You can track and A/B test almost all marketing channels, whether magazine articles, billboards, direct mail, social media posts, web pages or email campaigns. To do the test properly, make sure you have unique Trail-Scouts set up with unique offers or downloads, tracking telephone numbers, web forms, analytics and unique email addresses, so the full picture can be seen.

From that position you are ready to start A/B testing: put together two versions of the piece of marketing and track the results for each. You then use the winner for the majority of your promotion until you come up with another element to test and improve upon; then run another A/B test.

When these small changes are used many times throughout the year, they can add hundreds of additional business enquiries and therefore thousands to your bottom line.

4. How to create Big Fish / Little Fish Partnership Success

When I set up my video, audio and photography business – Yomp VAP – I wanted to get exposure very quickly, but I knew that start-up costs for this type of business was always going to be relatively expensive, with camera equipment, studio hire, staffing, etc. So with a fresh marketing challenge laid down (I wish I was a bit easier on myself sometimes) I decided I wanted to make the biggest splash I could within the first week to see if I could recoup much of my investment in that period. Imagine that – a fully operational business which was profitable within the first week with all its start-up investment paid back.

To do this the usual strategies like HQ website creation, e-mail marketing and company branding were immediately started, but although these digital techniques can deliver business enquiries quickly, I would still need to generate the leads, warm them up, meet with them, pitch, quote, book the photography or video shoot date and then complete the work before being paid. This is required foundation work for all businesses, but I like the-one week challenge to really help kick start the new business.

So how did I do it?

The answer is through a strategic partnership with an established businesses. I call this the Little Fish / Big Fish Partnerships Method – ideal for small businesses or businesses looking to develop into new markets or launch new products (the Small Fish).

For Yomp VAP I needed access to small business owners within the local area who were:

Thinking about themselves and their business

Well presented

Ready to commit money there and then for video or photography work.

I started by looking online at business conferences for that week through eventbright.com. I knew the first job for Yomp VAP had to be manageable so I filtered by numbers of attendees, not wanting them to be in the hundreds but not in single digits either.

I found a Micro-Conference on 'Building Outstanding Businesses' by an excellent speaker, David Norris of the Business Doctors (my Big Fish). I met with David and pitched the idea of offering free corporate headshots for all his attendees at the Micro-Conference.

He loved it because he had a couple of days to use it as a marketing tool to push for a few more attendees; for me, the beauty of this arrangement was that Yomp VAP instantly reached large numbers of highly qualified prospects through the massive endorsement of the established business, David's Business Doctors.

David also changed the Eventbrite description to promote the free headshots from Yomp VAP (nice free advertising again). The local Chamber of Commerce had agreed to email their thousands of members about the event the day after I met with David, so he was really excited about the value add we were supplying. He actually put it as the second sentence in the promotional email the Chamber of Commerce sent out as well as a main feature of his emails going to his database.

On its third day of existence Yomp VAP was being endorsed to thousands of businesses owners in the local area without having taken one commercial photograph or video as a business!

Day five was the event. Mike, my lead photographer, was onsite; he set up a photo booth at the back of the conference room, using nothing more than his professional camera and four lights on tripods and a white pull-down backdrop on a stand. With the small amount of start-up kit we had procured in the previous four days, it looked highly professional.

Soon the attendees started to arrive and David was an incredible host. You could tell he had conducted many conferences and knew exactly how to work a crowded conference room, meeting everyone and mingling.

At the end of David's Micro Conference, he told everyone how important profile pictures are for modern social media and that today they were all in luck as they had the opportunity to get an excellent free one taken by Mike. He went on to say that the modern small business should also have a regularly updated YouTube channel and use the power of video or even audio through podcasts; if they were interested in this then he was sure they would be in good hands booking a video shoot with Yomp VAP.

We had done it: David had been more than amazing and Mike soon had a queue. I went about booking video shoots with six of the attendees for the next few weeks, taking deposits upfront through our online payment system GoCardelss, to make sure we locked in the commitment and receive the cash we needed within the businesses first week.

The first week's Yomp VAP results were as follows:

24 Free corporate headshots = excellent Yomp VAP website portfolio and customer goodwill

6 corporate video bookings at £800 each = £4,800 invoiced on the fifth to seventh days of business

End result: total return on start-up cost investment, plus a small profit.

David had been willing to participate because it was a way to reward his loyal followers and customers without incurring any costs. Yomp VAP gained new customers, while the Business Doctors gained goodwill. I think that is what they call a win / win.

To take you through the process I have broken it down into steps, which can all be taken within the first week of business.

Outline precisely your target audience. You really need to know who your perfect customer is, and have the means to take action there and then. For us the people who did not buy where the employees of larger businesses as they had to go back to bosses, pitch the idea, get sign off, etc. which all kills momentum and defiantly will not yield results in the first week.

Find the partner, look for established local businesses that cater to a target audience similar to yours. Meet with them, show them how you can make them look good and only ask in exchange that you can simply be part of a joint product, event or even just an email to their database. Always focus on how you will make them look good to their customers; you are contacting them for help, not the other way around. Add massive value.

Supply the content for the partner to use; the last thing a busy established business owner wants is to start typing out paragraphs about you. By supplying the content you can also control how the benefits of your product or service are promoted. Obviously, work with them on any amendments they would like to make, after all they know their customers best, but always stay engaged in the process and never allow the partner to add things for you to do that you are unhappy to do or simply cannot deliver upon. I have had partners get carried away with what I am offering for free before and have had to rein them in as it is at my cost not theirs! Always clarify exactly what the offer is before it is sent out to the public.

Always know your follow-up strategy and never leave an opportunity hanging. If you have done all the hard work for free make sure you ask for the up-sell of the next logical step for the customer quickly so you get a return on investment ASAP. For customers who are not ready to buy the next logical step, stay engaged with them, ask for a quick testimonial, permission to use the work as a portfolio item or ask for a referral to a contact of theirs who is ready: everyone knows someone, so never let a contact who has tried your service go cold.

Put the Big Fish / Little Fish in your Digital TrailBlazer rucksack.

Whatever stage of business you are at, the likelihood is that you will launch a new product or target a new market soon. This method is the most effective way to access qualified potential customers and get amazing endorsements in the process. Best of all, you are building amazing strategic alliances for the future with established successful entrepreneurs and businesses who have spent years building their database.

5. Search Engine Optimisation (SEO)

SEO is the art of improving the visibility of a website in search engine results. It is focused on the unpaid 'organic' search results which are the top results listed in the main section on a search engine's results page.

This tactic is for our HQ website or for our OutPosts, if we focus on local or niche key phrases. The reason we love this tactic for finding new customers is that the higher ranked on the search results page your website is, and the more frequently it appears, the more visitors you will receive.

When surveyed, the majority of people expect brands at the top of search engine results to be the leading, most trusted brands on that chosen search term.

> 'Google isn't a search engine, Google is a reputation management system'
> CLIVE THOMPSON, WIRED MAGAZINE

It is therefore important to think about as many search terms related to your business as possible, and build a plan for getting better visibility across all of them. For highly competitive business sectors that can seem daunting, but despite the level of competition in search engine results there are always 'long tail' search terms to target.

Long tail search terms are three, four or even five word search terms, such as *'business insurance for lawyers'* or *'how much does an accountant cost?'*. The long tail phrases are not as competitive as shorter terms such as *'Business Insurance'* or *'Accountant'* and therefore many of your competitors will not be focusing on these longer terms. What they are missing is that anyone searching for either of these two long tail examples are in 'buying mode', so being at the top of Google for them is a quick win that good content on your web page could target to gain that traffic.

You need to focus on SEO as everybody uses search engines and as more people carry multiple devices this trend is only going to grow.

Knowing who you are targeting online then optimising your website's content for the keywords they are searching for is vital. Getting links from social media and other websites will give you the traction you need to climb up the rankings. This, however, is not a five-second job, but one that will be lasting and rewarding when you get it right. My advice is to educate yourself further about the process of SEO and then think about how you can create keyword-rich content that other business owners will want to link to.

Digital TrailBlazer basics of improving your search ranking

Now that you've built a great site, you'll want people to be able to easily find and visit your site.

Meta Data is the information that drives the page title and descriptions on a search engine's results page. This is vital content that Google uses to understand the intentions you have for your page. You can add your selected keywords into these areas. To do this look in your back end editor and find the place to edit the Meta

Title, Meta Description and Meta Keywords. If you are using WordPress for your website, I suggest downloading a plugin that does just this, such as Yoast SEO, which is free. Once you have found where to edit these, create compelling titles and descriptions that make people want to click and also have your keywords in. Do this for every page on your website.

Add your focused keywords throughout your webpage content. You won't get rankings for words that are not on your page, so include the words you want the page to rank for at least twice. Bear in mind that keywords are not magic: adding a keyword to your site does not mean search engines are going to find you just through that keyword.

Get a Google Webmaster account. Google is far and away the most important search engine and a Webmaster account can give you more insight into how they're ranking you.

Use page URLs that are relevant to search words and phrases. The name you give a page for its URL, for example **www.your website.com/your-keyword** , is really important. Why is this important? Because if a word is in your address it is seen as more relevant to your site by search engines. More relevant means more likely to show up in search results.

Use keyword phrases in your internal links on your website. If you link from one page of your website to another, use keyword-focused text for the link.

For example: To find out more visit our *Accountancy Surrey* page. 'Accountancy Surrey is clearly the focus for the SEO campaign and so the keyword is used to link to the page, rather than 'find out more'.

Use titles to headline content in your site (when appropriate). Search Engines see titles (which are tagged as H1, H2, H3, H4, etc.) as generally more important than regular text. You can add Titles to your site via your website's content management system, and they will usually be listed as H1, H2, etc. But don't write all your text in a title. That will make things worse for your site as it is not focusing on one specific phrase.

Is your site relevant only to people in a certain area? Highlight that by creating a Google Map that shows site visitors your location and by referring to the physical location of your business throughout the site where appropriate. Writing 'Visit our Guildford in Surrey office' is better than writing 'Come and see us.'

Use alt-text for your photos. This is a way of telling Google what the picture is about. Believe it or not, Google are not clever enough to look at pictures and understand exactly their relevance to the page – yet!

You can add alt-text to a regular picture by clicking on it and using the image editor to title the image, change the Alt-text and add a short description of the image. Use the keyword you want to focus upon within these sections where you can.

Get other sites to link back to your site. As a rule, the more sites that link to your site, the more Google trusts your website, especially if the websites linking to you are also trusted by Google. Think of other people linking back to your site as word-of-mouth that tells not just other people to check-out your site, but tells the search engines to do the same.

One point to note, not all links are equal, the more trusted the website the better, one link from the BBC or the Mail Online can be worth hundreds of small websites' links.

There is *nothing* more important to your ranking than other sites linking to you. To increase your links, build interesting content and let people know it exists. Just as building a business takes work, time and effort, building traffic to a website takes work, time and effort.

Link to your own site from any other sites you may have (like a Twitter or Facebook profile). If you have an email newsletter, archive it via your email provider's site so that your own newsletter acts as another site linking to you.

Maintain a blog. A blog enables you to continually add content to your site. The search engines like to see new content on your site.

Make reasonable goals. If you're a photographer, you are not going to show up at the top of the search results for the word 'photographer'. If you're a florist, you aren't going to show up at the top of the search results for 'flowers' or 'mother's day'. But if you're a photographer in Hampshire, you can potentially get to the top of the list for 'Hampshire Corporate Headshot Photographers'.

TRAILBLAZER MASTERY

A badly kept secret is that I *love* search engine optimisation and as a Digital TrailBlazer myself, I have a few other ways to get up the search engines super quick. To find out more go to **www.digitaltrailblazer.co.uk/mastery**

If you want more tips, do a Google search for 'SEO Tips'; there are many articles on this topic.

6. Direct Mail

When was the last time you received something 'remarkable' from a potential supplier through the post? I can think of only one occasions in the last three years.

The 'land' of 'your customer's door-mat' has moved full circle as the digital world has grown. It feels like all business marketing activity has moved online. Both effectively and ineffectively, this trend has developed an opportunity once again for direct mail.

We are looking to become *Digital* TrailBlazers, but to support that growth, don't rule out direct mail to drive traffic and conversions to your HQ, OutPosts and Scouts.

So back to the question: the one 'remarkable' piece of direct mail I received made me buy the item on offer, there and then…

One morning last year I gathered up the post sent to my office, threw away the usual pizza menus and special offers from the local hairdresser, placed the bank statements on my brother Tim's desk (you can always tell a bank statement from other post!) and what was left was one slightly yellow envelope, not dissimilar from the stereotypical international post you get from the USA. The envelope looked hand-written, but on closer inspection it was not – but I had already opened it by then (job one done by mystery sender).

When I opened the envelope I also found the internal letter was printed in a fairly realistic 'hand-written' font, but I read on because I had heard about this hand-written marketing technique before.

The generation currently coming out of universities and colleges have not owned homes pre-internet and therefore have not been the primary opener of 'junk mail'. This makes the old tactics the best place to start because they are a novelty and command attention.

I continued reading: the content itself was about businesses powering out of recession and the leadership traits needed to nurture staff to adapt to performing at a higher level during the new boom years.

As an employer (the letter's target market) I was interested and read two double sided pages of A4 all in hand-written font and laid out in a perfect traditional letter format.

At the back of the letter I found a separate, gold-coloured, high quality invitation to a conference in London. It was the mystery sender's conference on the subject. All I had to do was go online, activate the ticket and I was away.

As I had spent two minutes reading, I thought I would have a quick look further at the ticket proposition, so I typed in the URL given within the letter, found his landing page and video with more content on the conference, and I made the decision to spend the £89 activation fee for the ticket and attend the event – which was excellent.

Following the event, I now gratefully receive this man's marketing emails every month because I now 'know, like and trust' him. I have also attended two of his further events both considerably more expensive than the first one.

I would not have found that event through my usual online day-to-day routines, nor had I seen it anywhere else offline. But, I spent a decent ticket price for a half-day conference – as did another 200 people, so the event went well for the conference organiser too. It was a massive eye opener for me to not neglect offline activity to further drive online conversions.

As TrailBlazers I recommend that you use this method to effectively prompt action from your database, which might have gone a bit cold on you. I would also highly recommend this method for premium events you are looking to hold. If done properly it will have great effects upon your business, but like all marketing channels, do not go and spend silly money without understanding the facts. Add Trail-Trackers to it, such as a tracking phone number, unique Trail-Scout to drive visitors with a conversion form and a unique email address for quick conversions and easy access directly from the letter.

7. Email Marketing

People who do not embrace the marvels of email marketing often wonder what all the fuss is about. I often hear people say, 'My spam filter stops anyone email marketing to me, so why would it work if I email out?' And 'Isn't email outdated given blogs, social media, SEO etc?'

Wrong!

It allows targeting
....
It is data driven
....
It drives direct sales
....
It enables A/B testing
....
It builds relationships, loyalty and trust
....

It supports sales through other channels

It can be automated around web-user actions

Every email campaign you send out generates so much data that can be used for instant follow ups, market tracking, refining your message, looking at product popularity, feedback, building awareness, contribute to branding, strengthen relationships, encourage trust, cement loyalty and of course the most important – generating income.

So what makes a TrailBlazing email marketing campaign?

For services sector companies, it is all about giving your sales team warm leads to follow up, not just a list of people who have received an email. To do this, Digital TrailBlazers track the people who have opened the email, they also create Trail-Scouts directly designed to convert potential clients from being cold, to warm, to hot.

Each week or month they send out engaging email content to their database and within two to three days they produce two lists:

All the people who opened the email – warm leads.

All the people who have visited the landing page and filled in their online form (brochure download, 10 top tips article, event booking, etc) – hot leads

They simply follow up the activity from the two lists by calling the leads, putting them into their follow up process and getting busy converting them to sales.

The following graph shows your database being added into your email marketing software through the funnel at the top. Once your contacts are in the process they will be filtered using their activity on the email as the starting point.

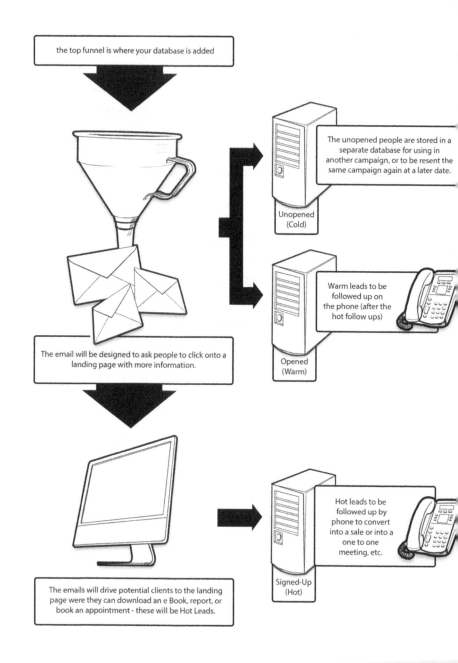

the top funnel is where your database is added

The unopened people are stored in a separate database for using in another campaign, or to be resent the same campaign again at a later date.

Unopened (Cold)

Warm leads to be followed up on the phone (after the hot follow ups)

Opened (Warm)

The email will be designed to ask people to click onto a landing page with more information.

Hot leads to be followed up by phone to convert into a sale or into a one to one meeting, etc.

Signed-Up (Hot)

The emails will drive potential clients to the landing page were they can download an e Book, report, or book an appointment - these will be Hot Leads.

The filtering starts with sending the email with the view to catch the eye of the reader with a quality headline focusing on the benefits to the reader for opening the email to read more. Then once the reader has opened it, the email will focus on engaging with him/her further and offering a link to a Trail-Scout that may have a special offer upon, an event invite or an e-book with even further high value free content.

Now this email has had time to create its reaction, two days later go back to your email report and pull out three lists:

The first is the people who did not open your email – these are the Cold database and are stored separately to receive another similar email at a later date to try and convert them with different headlines.

The second list are people who opened the email and did not click through to the Scout. These go into your Warm database and should be followed up by phone after the Hot leads.

The final list is the Hot leads who have visited your Scout and downloaded the material. These leads should be called within a maximum of 12 hours of them downloading you material.

This tactic is super successful when paired with well-trained telephone staff or an outsourced telephone follow-up service.

8. Attend networking events

The rise of business networking events has been astronomical in the last decade, with large American organisations bringing tried-and-tested breakfast meeting formats such as BNI, or dynamic new UK variations of the business breakfast meetings such as

4Networking, popping up all over the country. This format of meeting and promoting your services to other local businesses is an invaluable format to gain more customers.

A business networking event is a place where fellow business owners go to meet each other; it's a mixer and in most cases sociable as well as business-focused. Some events have formal referral-giving slots where business owners will actively pass business to each other and have their performance monitored and marked as a result. This is very targeted but quite full on and you have to be prepared to go out of your way to promote members of the group in order to show the value you can bring to the network.

Other formats, such as large 100+ attendee events that your local Chamber of Commerce, a trade show or the Institute of Directors might put on are more mingling events, where you need to be on your toes and circulating effectively if you do not want to be missing opportunities, stuck in a corner talking with one person all night.

As Digital TrailBlazers, we go to these events prepared with our 30-second elevator pitch which we will use over and over when the opportunity presents itself (usually triggered by someone asking, 'What do you do?'). An elevator pitch describes you, your business and how you help your target audience.

But never go networking expecting to sell; be friendly and listen, people buy from people – not from pushy sales machines.

9. Make genuine relationships on Social Networks

When I was at university, Facebook had just landed in the UK and we all flocked to it. Our only aims then where to see the photos from the night before or to catch up upon how the university rugby team had fared against the local rivals.

It was when I found a friend request from my mother that it all started to change!

We all have to tackle the questions:

What do I want to look like online?

How do I want to be portrayed across peer groups?

At that time I wanted my Facebook page to appeal to the girls' university netball team for my charm and good looks, but also to my mother 100 miles away to reassure her that I was eating well and did regularly shave!

Fresh out of university, I started my business and suddenly there was another factor to take into account: how much of me did my suppliers and customers need to see?

In the end, the first two were easily fixed in the end: I grew a beard and married one of the netball girls!

I then focused on becoming the business like entrepreneur online I was fast becoming offline. I still have my old photos available for my contacts to see the out-of-work me and I still look at Facebook for the rugby team's results and participate in many social conversation and forums. This is the beauty of a platform on which you can now reflect all aspects of your life in a balanced way.

We all need to understand these push and pull factors when taking ourselves and our business to the social networking space, but the relevance of my story is that being genuine and knowing what you're all about is fundamental to building relationships with your friends both offline and online.

When socialising with friends, nobody likes the 'Mr I Am'. I have been suspicious of people who feel the need to broadcast success story after success story. Maybe that's just my English attitude, but I grew up in an entrepreneurial family who came from very little and could easily brag about the trajectory of my father's and uncle's success. On the contrary, every genuine cash-in-the-bank multi-millionaire that I have ever met or worked with has been very unforthcoming about their own achievements. In fact, a common trait is a calm openness about success in response only to someone who shows a genuine interest and desire to learn from them. They do not open up to strangers or new acquaintances.

So be yourself, your true self and nothing else; look to make genuine friends through your online network, because it is this way that I have developed and converted hundreds of clients directly from social media activity.

For example, I have recently obtained 21 new clients from one Facebook post in the first month of launching a new Yomp Marketing SEO product. It was being promoted across all my marketing channels, but the lion's share of first month's sales came from posting the product's Trail-Scout into a Facebook private group.

There are many private and public groups to find on Facebook. Google+ and LinkedIn can also have the same effect in the right groups too.

I posted a quick update in the group about the new SEO product and asked if group members would be kind enough to give me some feedback. Within seconds I had had a spike in traffic to the Trail-Scout and the first couple of feedback comments were posted on the group's feed by other members. They responded to say that they loved the page design and the way it read, but some pointed out that an image needed repositioning, and another mentioned a sign-up form that slides down the page as you read would be useful. Their updates also concluded that they loved the product and that they might well have a contact that it would work for and could they forward the link to them. One of the members who gave great constructive feedback on the page design also signed up for three different campaigns for her websites in one go.

I was delighted with the uptake, especially as I was genuinely looking for constructive feedback upon the Trail-Scout from people I trusted and respected, and all of which I implemented and commented back on the original post, thanking them and showing them where their feedback had helped shape version two of the Trail-Scout.

This interaction meant even more comments on the one post, which in turn pushed the post higher up other people's Facebook feeds, which resulted in more traffic to the post, more clicks to the Scout, more feedback and subsequently more sales enquiries from people who read the page and believed in the product, me and my openness.

Most people also felt happy that I would deliver on my promises because I was an active member of their community and there would be an element of accountability to the group if I did not.

This type of success can only be driven through a good number of genuine relationships on social media. Even though you haven't met the person, if you have been genuine with them they may well give you some time to help improve elements of your marketing, then champion your cause if it is the right time and appropriate for them to do so. The more genuine relationships you have, the more likely and often this will happen for your brand.

This is how real viral marketing is started: your closest 300 contacts sharing to their closest 300 contacts, to reach millions.

10. Infographics

'Information graphics' – shortened to 'infographics' – are visual representations of information, data or knowledge intended to present information quickly and clearly.

They are well designed, visually appealing and can work as a stand-alone lead-generation tool for your TrailBlazing business.

Infographics have been around for many years, but recently the increase of a number of easy-to-use, free tools such as *Vizualize.me*, *Easel.ly*, *Piktochart.com* or *Infogr.am* have made their creation fast and simple.

Social media sites where users love images as much as text, such as Instagram, Pinterest, Facebook and Twitter, allow infographics to be spread among many people around the world.

Why do they work?

The eyes are an extension of the brain and well over half the population are visual learners. Businesses can benefit from understanding this and developing marketing messages within this visual graphic format.

Among the increasing noise online, your target market is demanding information and data that is quickly understood, clear, visually interesting, and easily shareable. The speed with which you can share an infographic is the beauty of the medium. Website or blog visitors are far more likely to forward to their followers an image than a written blog post.

Key elements to a successful Infographic

With these elements in place, you will be on course to creating a great lead-generating graphic for your business.

> **Short, sharable, and accurate title** – I recommend no more than 70 characters in length as you will want the title to be in a large font and to stand out at the top of your image.

> **Data that makes sense together** – Think of an infographic as telling a story through quotes, statistics and data. Pick a service or a market you operate in and tell a story that works with your business. 'The History of CCTV' was a highly successful infographic we put together for CCTV installation company Maxtag, which netted them a number of new business enquiries from posting it on their HQ website, plus it was the most shared piece of content for them that year.

> **Colour scheme** – Maintain brand consistency for your colour scheme. If you are a blue, grey and white branded

business, make sure that your infographics align with this; having a pink and brown infographic will just look wrong on your blog or social media accounts. Adding another colour to your existing scheme to highlight important points is perfect, but as a base it needs to feel brand aligned.

Less is more – Using lots of small text will make it useless to mobile users who will not be able to read the small fonts. Also packing in hundreds of different statistics will detract from the clean, simple and quick for its reader ethos of an infographic.

Correct and current data – Having statistics from two years ago will make you look out of date, make sure you have current statistics and data.

Easy to share – Posting the original source of the infographic as an image on your blog will allow it to be shared and have its own image URL. From there it can be found in Google image searches, plus be easily embedded in other people's websites with a link back to you and easily be shared on social media accounts.

Why not try your first Infographic and see the buzz happen around it?

Here is one I prepared earlier:

Key Elements To A Successful Infographic

 SHORT, SHARABLE AND ACCURATE TITLE

DATA THAT MAKES SENSE TOGETHER

 COLOUR SCHEME

LESS IS MORE

 CORRECT AND CURRENT DATA

EASY TO SHARE

CHECK POINT 4 – DIGITAL TRAILBLAZERS 'TURN UP THE VOLUME' ON THEIR BUSINESS

At 4 a.m. on May 29, 1953, Edmund Hillary and Tenzing Norgay awoke in Camp Nine and readied themselves for their climb. Hillary discovered that his boots had frozen and spent two hours defrosting them.

The two men left camp at 6:30am. During this day's challenging climb, they came upon one particularly difficult rock face. This obstacle was the highest anyone had ever got to; all who had made it here had turned back or died trying to push on further.

Instead of turning back, Hillary committed to the challenge and stretched out every last ounce of his energy, resource and experience. By 10.15am he achieved yet another first and navigated a way past this seemingly impossible rock face, relentlessly pushing ever further up towards the summit.

The rock face remains known to this day as 'Hillary's Step'.

By month 10 of your 12-month climb you may be nearing your own Hilary's Step. You will have set up all your Digital Assets, you will have run campaigns through them, you have maximised the untapped and easiest to sell to resource, your current customers, so now it is time to take the leap of faith and tell the world…but how do you start?

Entrepreneur vs Company

As a Digital TrailBlazer, your personal brand (you!) is a big part of your business identity. Now that your business is starting to grow, so too must you as a personality and entrepreneur.

We are in the age of access all areas and if this makes you feel uncomfortable then you may find yourself falling short, stuck upon your 'Hillary's Step'. Everyone is looking for ways to stand out from the crowd and a clear personal brand focus that links your know-how with your company's message will create a strong point of difference from your competitors and, most of all, will help you get noticed for all the right reasons.

Your business has something they can never have – You!

Your business also has to have its own separate brand and Identity; this is important if you ever want to sell the business or empower marketing employees to communicate on its behalf. However, who are you more likely to follow closely on social media platforms? A person? Or a company?

If you are unsure, let me help you out.

Let's look at the current following of Richard Branson vs the colossal Virgin Group:

Richard Branson = 6,520,000 followers Vs. Virgin Group = 200,000 followers

He is a business celebrity of epic proportions, but what about a smaller UK Entrepreneur?

Let's take Brad Burton, founder of 4Networking, the business networking company I mentioned earlier who run 5,000+ events every year. Surely a company like 4Networking, who send this many event invitations to their vast database of members and potential members, would eclipse their founder?

Nope!

Brad Burton = 90,500 followers Vs. 4 Networking = 7,300 followers

I am sure you will agree that is an amazing difference, but what about a global service sector business? Australian entrepreneur and author Daniel Priestley, who co-founded Entrevo, creators of the Key Person of Influence business accelerator programme, which has trained 1,000+ entrepreneurs globally: surely this company is bigger than one of its co-founders?

Not likely…

Daniel Priestley = 13,500 followers Vs. Key Person of Influence = 3,250 followers

Focusing on your personal brand is so important as an entrepreneur. It really helps you engage on a personal level with your customer base. Once they know, like and trust you it is easy to gently direct them towards some of the marketing funnels we have set up in Check Points 1 or 2, and allow your business systems to convert the leads for you.

That is what great personalities do, they put themselves out there and develop intelligent sales and marketing systems to convert digital conversations into real customers.

So let's find out how we are going to get ourselves out there.

The Digital TrailBlazer 'Turn-up the Volume' Technique

My personal Twitter, Facebook, Instagram, Pinterest and other social media accounts, as well as the Digital TrailBlazer website, social media, blog, online course, this book and free weekly YouTube Training Channel, are the marketing areas that together have powered the growth of my business since I made the decision to expand beyond the Yomp Marketing website and actively seek a bigger audience.

Every week I receive emails and messages from new followers who found me on a Google search, social media or through my videos – proof that expanding beyond the blog was one of the best decisions I have ever made for both my personal brand and subsequently my companies lead generation. You may well be reading this book because of it.

From using the TrailBlazer 'Stretch Further' technique from the last Check Point, I get more eyes on my content and subsequently more enquiries. At this Check Point we now start to 'turn up the volume' within the marketing channels that we have stretched to. This way you work towards becoming an authority within your niche.

Turning up the volume online and offline is a technique that is not an interruptive, rude, capital letters in every tweet methodology – far from it. Turning up the volume in the busy online world is all about creating many little moments that when put together get you noticed again and again by your target audience. If you have become more prominent and more consistent across all the platforms you will boost traffic to your HQ, OutPosts and Scouts and the subsequent conversions, sales and brand awareness will slingshot you over your Hillary's Step and your final push for the summit of your Everest will be in sight.

10 Ways to 'Turn up your businesses volume'

1. Target obvious customers and places

Raising your profile can be as simple as putting yourself out there in the obvious places you did not considered available to you when you were a fledgling business. Ronnie Bartlett, who runs Albert Bartlett, his family's root vegetable business, says the company successfully raised its profile by targeting relevant media outlets.

> 'We featured in Good Food magazines around the world, as well as sponsoring the Food Channel and other food programmes,' he says.

It sounds simple, but why do 90% of us not do it? Recently I attended the Business Show in London and was surprised to see very few business service companies, such as accountants and IT support companies, exhibiting and speaking at the event. The few that did told me they had been inundated with potential customers, many of them had immediate requirements for help.

On a smaller investment scale, have you considered local events, parish magazines, post office windows or the local Chamber of Commerce networking events? I guarantee if your customers look at or attend these places then your competitors with a high profile will be there, so make sure you are too.

Like everything, track the return on investment, push them into Trail-Scouts or OutPosts and measure it to make sure it works for you before you spend thousands in the wrong places.

2. Champion a cause

Being associated with a related and relevant campaign or cause can be an excellent way to turn up your volume and network with other conscious, high profile players who also have an affiliation with that cause.

Kelvin Newman Director of Rough Agenda, an events company focusing on conferences and training, realised that not enough students were graduating with the skills many marketing agency employers needed in the online search space. They contacted a number of fellow digital agencies to support new courses within specific parts of the digital marketing skill set.

Through his championing and partnership with other leaders in the field, the UK is seeing many more digital marketing courses at university level and more companies helping with in-work placements.

As a result students are now better equipped and more in demand when graduating because of this specialisation.

In turn this has turned the volume up on Kelvin's businesses as all agencies and students are also more aware of him and his business and therefore regularly attend his conferences.

3. Consider marketing stunts

Stunts may be risky but they can be very effective if done in a witty and relevant way. Look at Richard Branson who kept on trying weird and wonderful challenges, most notably nearly writing himself off trying to circumnavigate the globe as a modern day Phineas Fogg in a hot air balloon. It may not have happened for him in terms of setting records, but it cemented him in our minds as a TrailBlazer of the skies and helped to promote his then newly formed airline.

Another entrepreneur, Ling's Cars founder Ling Valentine, put a missile truck on the side of the A1 motorway in the UK to promote her car-leasing firm. Yes you read correctly, I said 'missile truck'!,

When interviewed, Valentine commented:

> 'People's opinions changed from "you're mad" to "that's clever", she says. 'When Tony Blair (UK Prime Minister at that time) forced me to remove the rocket, I was inundated with messages asking where it had gone, and was interviewed on radio and TV.'

Valentine believes that putting herself in the firing line has been the most successful tactic to raise the profile of her business.

'Every other company in the car-leasing sector trades as a generic-style firm, such as XYZ Leasing, but I trade as myself. People know who they're dealing with,' she says.

When a stunt like this coincides with an important message you want to share, such as a new service launch or a new location / branch opening, it can be extremely successful at gaining brand awareness and PR.

For Yomp Marketing, Tim (my brother and co-founder) and I sponsored our father Dennis Woods to walk to the South Pole on the centenary of one of the Victorian eras greatest TrailBlazers. In 1911, the Norwegian explorer Roald Amundsen led a successful expedition and won the race to become the first human to stand upon the southernmost point on earth, the South Pole.

This stunt was highly relevant to the launch of our new Digital TrailBlazer online course and an exciting challenge that we reported back to all our clients.

The definition of the word 'Yomp' is 'To march whilst fully equipped over challenging terrain', The Antarctic does not get much tougher!

The stunt was great 'volume turning up' material, with the Yomp Marketing flag flying over the South Pole, the subsequent online and newspaper coverage – and of course we were able to assist a life time dream trip for the old man!

4. Display advertising through Google

Google's display network is massive, encompassing more than 4 billion daily page views, 700 million monthly users, and reaching more than 80% of the online audience. However, I can guarantee you that your competition are not even using it, yet alone mastering it.

Google Display network is not the pay-per-click adverts at the top and right hand side of the Google search results. It is a group of more than a million websites, videos, and apps that allows Google to place third party adverts automatically on their websites. These are the usually flashing adverts on the right hand side of blogs and directories, or the pop ups on YouTube videos, to give a few examples.

The Display Network is one part of the Google AdWords Network and is managed in the same login area as your AdWords campaign. Through the Display Network your adverts can be automatically matched to websites and other placements like mobile phone apps, when your keywords are related to the sites' content. You can also choose to target specific sites, pages about specific topics, demographic groups, and more.

To show your ads on the Display Network, set your ad campaign to 'Display Network only' or 'Search Network with Display Select'. As I've mentioned, Google estimates that their display network provides coverage to over 80 percent of all internet users, which is one massive reason why you should be using it. However, it's not just the reach of the network that makes it so impressive, it's the ability to target users in a variety of ways that makes the Google Display Network such a potentially lucrative platform for advertisers.

Different types of display adverts

It is a common misconception that the Display Network only provides you with the option of displaying image ads. In fact, the Google Display Network lets you advertise in a variety of formats and sizes with text ads, static and animated image ads, rich media and video ads.

Text Ads – Google allows you to run the same text ads on display as you would on the pay-per-click search network. Text ads consist of a headline and two lines of text, and allow advertisers to create a range of ads to test which version is generating the most clicks.

Image Ads – A static image that would fill the entire ad block on the website it appears on. You can include custom imagery, layouts and background colours on image ads.

Rich Media Ads – Rich Media Ads include interactive elements, animations or other aspects that change depending on who is looking at the ad and how they interact with it. For example, a moving carousel of products.

Video Ads – Video ads have become more popular since YouTube was included on the Display Network. You can now use AdWords to place your ads next to YouTube videos

The Display Network offers a tremendous amount of targeting options and control. However, if you don't find an offer that works across it, then you will end up wasting money and come to the conclusion that the Display Network doesn't work. This is rarely the case and is usually a sure sign that your offer is not right or the group you are targeting is not correct.

Remember, we are steering your target audience to click through from your adverts to your Scouts, Outpost or HQ; from there it is all about how well your web asset converts the website visitor.

5. Sponsored social media updates

Now that you have been able to stretch your communication across the main social platforms your audience is hanging out on, we want to drive the volume of engaged audience members to all the excellent content you are posting on these platforms. To 'shout louder' on social media and communicate outside your immediate following and circles, the main social media platforms offers distribution channels for the promotion and amplification of your content.

To stand out above the mass of noise on the Facebook, LinkedIn and Twitter crowds, and train the right eyes onto their content, Digital TrailBlazers invest a small budget to boost their social media reach. We do this to optimise the work that we put into promoting ourselves and our business and if that work is only seen by a small number of people who already know us, then we are not stretching ourselves properly and shouting our loudest.

If you're thinking, 'But social media is supposed to be open and free!' you would be correct, but it is open and free to millions of others and we have to get your message seen above all of them. As a Digital TrailBlazer, you will be using conversion techniques, such as specially created Scouts with compelling e-books, or special offers, to produce a return on investment from your social channels, so spending budget to put your audience through this conversion process is a wise decision.

Let's look more closely at some of the main platforms and how we can grow our audience and as a result increase our conversions:

Facebook sponsored updates

Now that Facebook has joined the dark side and floated on the Stock Exchange there is more pressure than ever on Zuckerberg and his team to deliver a quarter-on-quarter increase in profitability to their shareholders. I am glad that they made this decision, as Facebook needed the financial backing of the City for its long term growth outlook.

What does this mean? – There has been a well-documented decline of 'brand pages' and there updates within peoples time lines. There simply is so much noise and people have on average 500+ friends and are liking so many pages that that it was becoming unrealistic to show all of a company's posts in a person's timeline.

This means two things for Digital TrailBlazers:

- Engage with users as a person and connect with as many people as possible to work in tandem with your company page as a power-using entrepreneur.
- Facebook is quickly becoming a pay-to-engage network for brands and companies.

As Digital TrailBlazers, we use Facebook's self-serve advertising platform to hyper-target key audiences. It really is amazing how targeted you can be, and this is simply the biggest and most important asset to harness on Facebook.

You can drill down from countless drop-down menus and search bars to choose a target audience by their age, sex, location, level of education, interests in certain sports or music genres, you can even target people who have liked your competitors' pages. This gives us a really clear and direct way to get our content, and therefore our conversion tactics, out there and converting like never before.

As a complementary benefit to this type of advertising, there is the increased exposure and brand awareness for the target audience member you are nicely and politely following across the social platforms and beyond, offering them relevant engaging content. They may not click on your advert, but they will see it and have a conscious or even subconscious thought about you, which could make all the difference in the future.

Twitter sponsored updates

As most of us know, Twitter is getting noisy: there are over 500 million tweets sent each day. But Twitter is only as noisy as you allow it to be, and as a Digital TrailBlazer, following thousands of people is not the best use of your time. You simply cannot keep up with everyone and eventually you will just make lists of people you consider close contacts and then only view this list when looking to engage through Twitter. So why follow thousands of people in the first place?

A business coach recently sat with me and announced that he had over 40,000 followers on Twitter. I was impressed: a Digital TrailBlazer with an engaged online following that rivals most premiership football players is quite an asset for marketing too. When he left my office I looked him up and found that he did have the followers he claimed, but was following over 55,000 people himself. On top of that, he had only sent 2,500 tweets; to grow an audience of that level with such a small number of updates is extremely difficult if you were not already famous.

This chap was apparently not famous. Other than a badly kept website with a few posts on a blog, there was no real sign of him online. His tactic of following anyone he could find online was all that had netted him an ever-increasing number of followers; worse still, on inspection there were a number of 'ghost profiles' among his followers – the sort of profiles that are computer-generated and their following is sold to Twitter users who want big fake followings.

This immediately placed him in my mind as an un-authentic, unconfident in his own message Twitter user; more than that, I mentally labelled him as a spammer and certainly could not ever recommend him to any clients that I work with. In fact from this five-minute research into him, I could tell that he was not someone who I would want to work with and declined to work on the SEO for his website – which had been the original reason for our meeting.

This business coach was not a bad person, but through bad advice or just trying to 'game' social media he demonstrated untrustworthiness online which we, as Digital TrailBlazers, need to learn from. It is far better to have a profile that has more followers than people you follow as it shows an audience built through what you say, not by people's tendency to follow back.

So what is the quickest way over and above organic Twitter posts, that we can increase our followers quickly through what we say and the value we offer?

The answer is Twitter's Lead Generation Cards. These large promoted tweets combining image, text and call to action are like embedding a Trail-Scout into the body of a tweet. For your target audience, which again can be selected through drop-down audience demographics, they are simple, one-click opt-ins for e-book downloads, claiming offers, or registering for your latest webinar/event.

They have a great return on investment if used in conjunction with a Trail-Scout, and of course spreads that all important brand awareness.

LinkedIn sponsored updates

LinkedIn is the natural home for some TrailBlazers as it is all about business, all of the time. If your brand is targeting other business professionals, LinkedIn advertising offers a number of products to boost conversions and drive traffic.

Sponsored posts pull images from the source links, so you will want to make sure your Scouts have decent imagery to pull through. You can add images on other forms or sidebar LinkedIn adverts, but I have found that the sponsored posts get more conversions than the side bar ads.

What I like about the LinkedIn advertising platform is that it will let you launch multiple versions of the same ad to see which one proves most effective. This can help you test different combinations of headline, description, image and landing page to see which are the most fruitful.

Like Facebook and Twitter this is also great for brand awareness and goes a long way to 'stretching' and shouting louder' about the massive value you offer your audience.

Conclusion to sponsored social engagement

Remember that the social networks are distribution channels and increasingly display ad networks, so you have to put a little budget to one side to engage with qualified target audience members, attract their attention to your content and give massive value in order to convert more and more prospects. Done well, you will be surprised by the power of putting your head above the noise parapet and shouting that little louder through social media.

6. Publish a Book

You're reading this book – thank you.

I have been able to successfully reach out to you and perhaps even convince you to look further into other content on my website or YouTube channel. Perhaps we may even work with each other one day, or maybe we already are.

Becoming a published author, whether through traditional, hybrid or self-publishing, shows that you have a clear idea of what you are about and you have attractive ideas that are worth sharing.

You have a published voice.

Digital TrailBlazers can attract opportunity to themselves as an author and in turn get speaking, media and PR opportunities because of it. The distribution of your book can be automated and on online platforms, notably Amazon – which is also one of the biggest search engines in its own right.

Many entrepreneurs publish books or even white papers on Amazon's Kindle Direct Publishing (KDP). Although for real volume turning up, a print book has even more power.

Authors are generating some income from their efforts, but even more importantly for Digital TrailBlazers, more are seeing an increase in traffic to their HQs and subscribers to their social channels. Many of their books are ranking high in Google for competitive keywords related to their topic, which again bring new audiences and created further lead generation.

Let's face it, a book is the best and most compelling business card available; it will help you stretch further and louder on and offline.

As Benjamin Franklin once said:

> 'Either write something worth reading or do something worth writing about.'

7. Be transparent

Today's consumers are demanding more information about the products they buy and the companies that supply them. Tapping into this buying trend and can help give your business a far better profile.

Take South of England based restaurant The Pig'. Chef James Golding, whose two key lieutenants aren't his sous chefs but his forager and his kitchen gardener, offers an uncomplicated and simple British garden food menu influenced by the forest and coast. They have a large food garden where most products come from right in front of diners' eyes, and anything non-garden growable is sourced locally and transparently.

> 'What can't be grown in our kitchen garden, or in
> the extensive vegetable and fruit beds, is
> sourced locally – our further commitment
> to the 25 mile menu.'
> **JAMES GOLDING**

Their website tells you the name of the grower or farmer with details about each.

A second example is from the online training world, an entrepreneur named Pat Flynn. Pat is so transparent when teaching people how to make money online, he writes detailed reports about his own online earnings.

> 'I always begin by describing the things I did within
> the previous month that might have an impact on
> my income. Then I breakdown the sources of my
> income to the cent and always finish
> with what I've learned.'
> **PAT FLYNN**

These reports have been the most popular and helpful posts on his blog, landing him a book publishing deal and expenses paid speaking gigs in the US, UK and Australia.

So what can you talk about openly with your clients that will impress them and become a destination piece of content for new followers? Some examples might be a customer testimonial on a third party website where you cannot edit the bad testimonial (if you have any) like tripadvisor, checkatrade or Yelp. Or what about 'our process' pages to show exactly how you deliver your service.

8. Podcasting

Well-conceived podcasts are an effective, portable, convenient and intimate way to deliver your content. It is also fantastic for building ongoing relationships with your audience.

The definition of a podcast is a digital audio file made available on the internet for downloading to a computer or portable media player, typically available as a series, new instalments of which can be received by subscribers automatically.

Most audiences use smart phones to subscribe and I listen to many podcast shows in a week while at the gym, driving or walking the dog. The regular output makes it one of the best forms of engagement – it's basically your own radio show.

Podcasts make information personal. In a podcast, the content is communicated directly to you, the listener, either verbally or through video. That's a much more intimate way of getting information than reading it from an e-mail or document and your audience will feel they know you at a far deeper level.

Podcasts are convenient and easy to consume. – Once you subscribe to a podcast feed, new podcasts are automatically downloaded to your computer as soon as they are available. Your audience can therefore listen to them at their convenience.

Podcasting is a time-efficient form of communication. – You can listen to podcasts while you do other things at work or at home, or during your commute.

Podcasts are portable. Once a podcast is on your smart phone you can take it with you and listen whenever or wherever you want.

Podcasting is an on-demand technology. Listeners decide what they want to hear, and when they want to hear it. On the one hand, this means you're competing for their ears. On the other hand, it means that if they are subscribing to your podcasts there's an excellent chance they're actually getting the information you are providing to them.

Podcasts are one way to deliver on a social networking strategy. Your podcast subscribers are the core of your community and over time they will be your best prospects for deepening the relationship through cross-sell and loyalty tactics.

The best way to understand the potential for podcasts is to tune in and watch or listen to podcasts of interest to you. Then think about your subject matter and how you will be able to harness this powerful marketing tool.

9. Online Video Channel

Creating an online video channel for your service sector business is a powerful and under-used branding tool. It helps launch your company to a larger engaged audience and it increases your websites' SEO in an inexpensive and simple to create way.

In a similar way to Amazon helping you promote your e-books and printed books, video channels such as Vimeo or YouTube help to promote your videos online.

YouTube has 80% of its traffic originating from outside the U.S. Over one billion unique users access it every month and over six billion hours of YouTube hosted videos are viewed every month. This equates to roughly one hour of viewing time for every single person on Earth.

Every day, millions of new online business channels are subscribed to and the number of daily subscriptions has tripled. This does not mean the market is saturated; more adults aged 18 to 34 access YouTube than they do any TV network. For older demographics this is also growing, and with the increase in internet-enabled TVs, the age brackets that view online video content will grow even further.

As Digital TrailBlazers, we simply cannot ignore this market segment, but so far service sector companies have been the slowest to embrace it.

One of our TrailBlazers, UK accountant Jupp Castle, has used this medium to drive targeted traffic around specific events such as the UK Government's budget statements. These announcements, which happens twice a year, are vital for small businesses who may need to change tax rates or will incur increased levies on fuel, cost of employment or income tax, but they are delivered through two hours of a political speech.

Heather O'Rielly, the managing director of Jupp Castle, realised this opportunity and therefore shares her comments and thoughts on the Government's budgets via her YouTube Channel. She allows her unique personality and to the point manner to attract the type of audience that want bite-sized chunks focussed on their small business needs. She then backs this up with a business breakfast a couple of days later to discuss the implications of the new announcements and the opportunities they create. It is a fantastic example of targeted personality tied in with content marketing using online video as the driver towards specific Trail-Scouts and OutPosts to obtain event bookings.

You don't need to hire a professional camera crew to get your point across. A smartphone, a tripod and some free video editing software will produce HD quality videos, at no cost. Take your mission statement, your brand and your vision and convey it loud and clear. You may not win an Oscar, but you will likely win over new followers when you turn up your marketing volume and post your videos on your HQ site and through social channels.

10. Marketing through speaking at events

Speaking engagements are great for turning up the marketing volume on your business. They give you a chance to personally interact with many prospective clients in one go, giving you a platform of authority and integrity that can only be achieved when you are the one standing in front of many others.

Speaking at events also gives your audience an opportunity to get a sense of your character and personality, factors that are often relevant to their decisions to work with you in the future. They also carry a public-spirited component as it's a great way to educate your target audience about your niche subject matter.

Finally, they also give you an opportunity to reach out to existing clients and reconnect by inviting them to hear your presentation.

When you speak you will be perceived as an expert and thus; speaking events can enhance your reputation and raise your visibility within your industry. When looking to get connected with event organisers and offer your services as a speaker (if you are not going to put the event on yourself), bear the following in mind:

Speaker Tips

Select your target audience – Don't go after everyone and anyone, decide what types of clients you want to target.

Locate the right event – Don't wait to be invited to speak, or you might find yourself waiting for ever! Once you've decided which audience you want to target make a list of all the events they would attend then systematically contact all the organisers offering your services.

Pitch an eye-catching topic – Try to identify timely or provocative topics that will attract the event organiser's eye but also ultimately your potential customers' attention and make them want to attend.

Those three steps should land you a couple of nice opportunities to speak at events, once you have them booked, here's how to prepare for the event:

Supporting marketing bumph – A speaking gig provides an opportunity to give away materials with your contact information to prospective clients. Consider handing out useful tools, such as presentation section headed notes, so the audience can follow along and take down their thoughts; or process checklists for them to take away and put into action. These interactive hand-outs will be used and therefore kept longer than your typical marketing collateral.

Help to promote the event and your talk – When it comes to publicising the event and the fact that you are brilliant enough to be invited to talk at it, all the TrailBlazer methods can be applied. Even if someone cannot go you can still use this as a great reason to contact them and show off your authority and credibility. The event organisers will love your efforts and you will be invited back.

At the event – Do not stand backstage, greet your audience at the entrance of the event and mingle with as many people as possible before your talk. It is always the personal touches that make people feel welcome and show off how cool and calm you are (even if you are not).

Leave time for questions – After your talk, take the time to answer two quick questions before the time slot finishes, then offer to answer any remaining in a break-out area afterwards. There you can also invite people to give you their business cards or drop them in a glass bowl at the back of the presentation area. Always have a couple of audience members ready to ask a question or two in case the rest of the audience is shy.

After the talk – Chances are, you won't have converted your audience into clients there and then. That's why the follow-up to your talk is so important. Always be sure to record your presentation, even if you do it with your own, hand-held digital recording device. That way, you can make recordings available to participants as a courtesy and also distribute the presentation for marketing purposes later on. Follow up with everyone who handed over a business card or expressed some interest in your service. List your talk on your website and on all other channels so you can maximise your exposure.

As with any other marketing tool, a single speech will not always set your world alight, but it will give you masses of confidence, contacts and further marketing material. It will also create a platform to push on from and turn your volume up further. So, make speaking events a regular part of your marketing portfolio and it will help attract clients and enhance your reputation.

TRAILBLAZER MASTERY

For a bonus eleventh turn up the volume tactic, think about entering local and national business / entrepreneur awards. Yomp and its clients have had great success with this tactic in the past. Go to **www.digital-trailblazer.co.uk/mastery** for access to a list of business awards.

CHECK POINT 5 – THE FINAL PUSH TO THE TOP

'The special forces gave me the self-confidence to
do some extraordinary things in my life. Climbing
Everest then cemented my belief in myself.'
BEAR GRYLLS

After readying themselves and conquering the seemingly impossible Hillary's Step, the two-man-team made the final push to the top of their mountain.

The final months of your 12-month climb is the most important. You will have put most of the first four stages together and it may look and feel a bit disjointed and perhaps messy; you may even be looking at your figures and thinking that it will not happen.

Don't worry this is normal.

Now is the time to get back to the plan and assess where you are on your Trail-MAP. Of course you will have been doing this at least every month, but this is the last deep dive into the plan.

Look at the figures and the marketing channels, find where the success is coming from and really pile time and investment into those areas because this will be your best chance of getting that all important, final momentum to get to the top within your time limit.

Sit down with your Summit Team and work out if there are any millimeters of improvements to be made, or costs to be cut so you can use the savings as profit straight to the bottom line, or better still as the investment that is required to catalyst the final enquiries that will make a good year into a TrailBlazing year.

Give your Summit Team an Everest-worthy motivational speech

When you sit down with your Summit Team in this Check Point Five meeting, give them your best motivational speech. This is your Everest and if as a team you hit the summit you will all be going out to celebrate in style, so remind them of that and any bonuses or incentives that you have tied in with performance.

Now is the time to go for it, it is the last push and you can see the snowy peak almost in your grasp.

Go on, get up there!

At 11.30am on the 29th May, 1953 Edmund Hillary, the beekeeper from Auckland, and Tenzing Norgay, the Sherpa from North India, reached the summit of Mount Everest. Hillary reached out to shake Tenzing's hand, but Tenzing gave him a hug in return.

Writing of their final push to the summit, Hillary reflected:

'Another few weary steps and there was nothing above us but the sky. There was no final pinnacle. We looked round in wonder. To our immense satisfaction we realised we had reached the top of the world.'
EDMUND HILLARY

The two men enjoyed only 15 minutes at the top of the world because of their low air supply, but they spent their time taking photographs, delighting in the view, placing a food offering (Tenzing), and looking for any sign that the missing climbers from 1924 had been there before them (they didn't find any).

Hillary and Tenzing have become legend.

Celebrating properly

'A business has to be involving, it has to be fun, and it has to exercise your creative instincts.'
RICHARD BRANSON

After reaching the top and celebrating together, the two men climbed down the mountain to rejoin their team at the last check point. From afar, they looked so exhausted that team leader Colonel John Hunt assumed they had failed to reach the summit, but then the two climbers pointed to the mountain and signaled they had reached the top and there were celebrations all round.

It is essential that you do not forget to celebrate your achievements. You may be exhausted from the late nights and early mornings needed for success; you may have had to make sacrifices and push your team and family. You may have lost your rag and stamped your feet (I know I do at times) but that is all ok so long as during the process you are respectful, and when you hit your 12-months' target who wants to celebrate on their own?

Go to the people that have worked so hard for you, the friends and family that have supported you and also your customers who have helped to make it happen and celebrate.

Organise an event to mark the occasion, or at the very least send personalised Thank You's of some type to all important members of your team. It is really important to reward the people around you and be grateful for the success you have, because when you are back out on the mountain range next year you will once again need them and they will remember the small and the big things from last year that have made them want to keep on supporting you.

There is of course one last person to thank, and that is you.

Without you this would not have happened, your family would not be in the position you have created for them and perhaps your children would have not had the future they will now because of your blood, sweat and tears. Go out and treat yourself to something and make sure it is 100% a treat because of the success you had last year in business. This way you can look at it (if it's a thing) or think back to it (if it's an experience or holiday) and remember how good it felt and how much you want it again and again.

These treats and celebrations are the motivation that gets average Digital TrailBlazers over their Hillary Steps to become world beating Digital TrailBlazers. Never leave out this step, it is the most fun!

New Frontiers

When their 15 minutes were up, Hillary and Tenzing began making their way back down the mountain. It is reported that when Hillary saw his friend and fellow New Zealand climber George Lowe (also part of the expedition), Hillary said, *'Well, George, we've knocked the bastard off!'*

News of the successful climb quickly made it around the world; both Edmund Hillary and Tenzing Norgay became heroes.

Finding your next Everest

As Digital TrailBlazers we know that each year we look up from the foothills of our mountain range and see our business growth mountain. The one we look at should always be our Everest; we should never settle for lower expectations than the previous year. Therefore we plan our Everest ascent every year.

This was the same for Hillary, who went on to lead numerous other expeditions over the next two decades, including journeys to the South Pole, six Himalayan ascents, a search for the fabled Yeti and the source of the Yangtze River. He led the New Zealand section of the Trans-Antarctic expedition from 1955 to 1958, and in 1958 participated in the first mechanised expedition to the South Pole.

He never settled for the one standout year, he kept on going back to the coal face

again and again.

Don't forget, by this stage you have just climbed the most amazing mountain of your business career. You have systems in place that have automated how you can generate business enquiries and when the enquiries become customers you know how to sell even more to them. You have an ever-growing profile both online and offline so it is about time you found your next Everest.

The first piece of advice here is do not worry, you will be on such a high from achieving the goals you have set for yourself that you will be raring to go. If you have not quite made it over your Hillary's Step in the last 12 months, then also do not worry, I guarantee that if you have followed even 50% of the advice in this book, you will be further ahead than you would have been without the work you have put in.

So now take stock of where you are once the celebrations have finished and start the process again. Re-establish your BaseCamp and start to perfect the models and planning strategies you went through 12 months ago. Make sure you are again realistic and

CHECK POINT 5 - THE FINAL PUSH TO THE TOP

bring in as many opinions as you feel are appropriate to construct the next Trail-MAP.

Make sure you have a clear route to the top of your newest mountain. Prepare yourself and your Summit Team. Get your boots back on your feet, start up towards Check Point 1 and get even better at selling to your existing customers.

Great work, Digital TrailBlazer!

FINAL THOUGHTS AND MAKING IT HAPPEN

On the death of Edmund Hillary on 11th January, 2008, New Zealand Prime Minister Helen Clark said:

> 'Sir Ed described himself as an average New Zealander with modest abilities. In reality, he was a colossus. He was a heroic figure who not only "knocked off" Everest but lived a life of determination, humility, and generosity.'

As Digital TrailBlazers we have to take inspiration from this because to be able to effectively sell more, find new customers and turn up the volume online, we will need to be able to win friends and gain trust and support.

Hillary's modesty was the right method for him. You may be a different character type, but always be likable and approachable even when you are a 'colossus'.

Putting it all together

Creating the systems explained in this book will provide a way to see how your customers contribute to the bottom line, both individually and collectively. The simple processes, measuring tools, formulas and equations put into your business will immediately show an exponential growth of customers, which is both informative and inspiring to everyone within the business.

These easy to understand numbers demonstrate the power and potential for explosive profitability. Double the number of leads within a single month and chances are that profits will also double.

Celebrate the seemingly miraculous progress, savour it, learn from it and be energised and motivated as a team. Then multiply the one-month effort by a dozen and everyone will begin to have a vision of unlimited potential, possibility, performance, and profits.

Within just a few weeks, any business thinking small and feeling stagnant can become a TrailBlazer visionary business thinking big and reaping incalculable rewards with refreshed momentum, confidence and tangible equity.

That business I know will be yours – good luck!

TAKE ACTION – YOUR NEXT STEPS

My recommendation for all businesses wanting to tackle their Everest in the next 12 months is to check out the following resources and get involved with the Digital TrailBlazer community. I would love to hear how you are getting on and also to meet you at one of our networking events or conferences.

The Digital TrailBlazer free training videos –
www.DigitalTrailblazer.co.uk/free

The Digital TrailBlazer online learning course –
www.DigitalTrailblazer.co.uk/the-course

The 'Done for you' Digital TrailBlazer Campaign –
www.DigitalTrailblazer.co.uk/done-for-you

ABOUT THE DIGITAL TRAILBLAZER 'DONE FOR YOU' PROGRAM (BY APPLICATION ONLY)

Anyone who has attempted to reach the summit of Everest will have almost certainly been accompanied by Sherpas – elite mountaineers with an expert knowledge of their surroundings and the challenging terrain ahead.

Sound familiar? Allow us to guide you towards the summit of your Business Growth Mountain.

The Digital TrailBlazer Programme

A rigorous selection process – not everyone makes it to the starting point

12 Month Return on Investment

Monthly Campaign Meetings with all team members to collaborate on new ideas and present previous months results

More marketing and business growth skills than you could recruit for the same budget

Highly skilled and experienced people to bounce ideas off

Regular accountability to keep your business on track

Time out of your business to work on your business

All activity is tracked for return on investment

...and a side order of fun!

If you are interested in working with your very own team of business Sherpas, you need to head over to **www.DigitalTrail blazer.co.uk/done-for-you** right away to download the TrailBlazer pack.

Or read on for a current TrailBlazer Programme Case Studies:

CASE STUDY - JUPP CASTLE ACCOUNTANCY

Written by Heather O'Reilly, Managing Director of Jupp Castle, for her application for the Inspire Businesses Awards (which she went on to win).

Heather took on the TrailBlazer Done For You Program and was able to overcome her challenges in the following ways:

How did Jupp Castle add significant value to their clients and improve service offerings, client focus, marketing effectiveness and innovation?

Our Challenges were:

How to break the stereotype of typical accountants without losing professionalism and move away from our traditional brand without losing client base and the essence of the business.

How to move away from hourly-based pricing to offer clients a flexible fee structure with fixed fees and customisable packages

How to become an integral part of clients businesses for owner managed SMEs

How to focus on growing clients' businesses rather than giving them just compliance and reporting

How to help clients minimise time spent on admin and book keeping

Setting up internal processes to ensure that work is completed consistently and on time, providing visibility and information to assist with providing excellent client service.

The objective was to create a new company brand that was strong, fresh and unique. A brand that could be instantly recognised. We understood that this was not something we could do alone and so joined forces with a local company Yomp Marketing as we are always keen to use local talent.

We now have a new forward-thinking brand and website which portrays the accounting practice as it really is. We have developed a series of new packages which have been created to address needs based on client feedback. These packages mean that we can assist business owners on every level from book keeping to financial director services. This develops a better understanding of our clients' businesses and means that we help them achieve their goals.

From client surveys we understood that one of the biggest challenges for business owners was the burden of administration and book keeping. We therefore looked at the whole of market to see which products were available to help reduce time spent on this aspect of running a business. We found Xero, a cloud based software, to be the best available and have become Xero partners. All the staff have now been trained and certified in the product so they are able to assist clients at every stage.

We have since 'No-Brainier upsold' over 60 clients to Xero and are able to help them with their day-to-day administration remotely, which saves them both time and money.

Every process within the firm now has a procedure to ensure that, with the correct level of knowledge any task can be carried out consistently. We have also set up a CRM for sales leads and prospects to help us track our sales pipeline and measure our performance in winning new clients, which is essential to the growth of the business.

Our business plan shows targeted growth of 12% per annum on recurring fees which will be achieved by offering additional services to current clients and winning new clients. We can now offer new services such as legal services which includes will-writing, powers of attorney and arbitration and mediation.

We have already established a financial services arm to the company as our aim is to be a one-stop shop for clients. We also have a full time IFA who can offer the whole range of market advice on pensions, protection, mortgages and investments.

Staff are offered incentives to introduce new clients to the business by way of commission. Their professional development and training is constant with encouragement and support for any qualifications which will benefit both them and the business.

We also put on regular social activities both in and out of work time with an annual day out in the summer. This year we will be having our first family Christmas party for both staff and clients with entertainment for the children and an opportunity for clients to meet with both the team at Jupp Castle and other clients within informal surroundings.

The team have all been given their own business cards and are encouraged to give them out wherever possible; they are also free to attend networking events during working hours.

We have begun to use social media much more to heighten our profile as we realised that this was the way to reach young entrepreneurs and business owners. We write a weekly blog to keep clients informed of any changes in legislation and other information that may be useful.

After the success of our breakfast seminars on an Introduction to Xero, we are planning additional seminars this year on Growth Accelerator, which is a government funded scheme with matched payments for coaching and management training and also a seminar on peer-to-peer funding. We feel that so many business owners are unaware of the help they can get to grow their businesses and by running such seminars, we can help them in this process. We will also be running auto enrolment seminars next year to help small business owners understand their obligations under the work place pensions legislation and Xero workshops to give more detailed guidance on how to use the software.

With our new CRM system tracking prospects and leads, we now have a process that ensures that reminders are sent to individual members of the team to send quotes and follow up emails for all prospects.

We send a monthly email newsletter to all clients and contacts to inform them of any relevant changes in legislation. We want to constantly develop our offering to clients and prospects and we have produced a free e-book download for the website called *The*

A –Z of how to build a better business, which is available on our HQ website now.

We are also designing a quick quote InfoSwap tool for our website so that prospects who want just year-end accounts can, by answering a few simple questions, get a quotation for services instantly.

By constantly adding these different services we hope to differentiate ourselves from other providers and understand our clients' needs better.

How have Jupp Castle won new clients?

Champagne, chocolate and accountants! A fabulous launch event and ongoing marketing campaign for Jupp Castle's new company brand, website and service packages at The Elvetham Hotel in Hampshire.

This first marketing event of the year was oversubscribed by enthusiastic Hampshire business owners and it was a privilege to have in attendance Jo Fairley the founder and entrepreneur behind Green & Blacks Chocolate, as the guest speaker. The event created a wonderful opportunity for Jupp Castle to speak to clients about their new fixed price packages that they recently created to help win clients within their recently defined target audience of small to medium owner managed businesses in South East of England.

Jupp Castle also used this event to pitch Xero, the cloud-based online accounting software used within the new service packages.

Everyone enjoyed a glass of bubbly with some Green & Blacks chocolate, then Jo Fairley gave an insight into the phenomenal success story of Green & Blacks. You can watch the 2 minute event video here:

https://youtu.be/anWy60jnPxc

The target for the event was for people to gain greater awareness of Jupp Castle as a business, but also to promote Xero Accounting Software and the new Bronze, Silver and Gold accounting packages.

The event gave me (Jupp Castle's Managing Director, Heather O'Reilly) a window of opportunity to introduce the new company brand and packages to the excited audience just before I introduced Jo Fairley for her keynote slot.

After the event, follow-up workshops for taking new clients onto the Xero Accounting Software were promoted through email marketing campaigns, the new website, a search engine optimisation campaign and YouTube videos.

The Digital Marketing event follow-up resulted in 1,137 people engaging with the email campaign (clearly showing the wider interest in the videos and content produced from the event than just the attendees) and 69 people booked onto the workshops in March with the view to start migrating onto the Xero Accounting Software and as a consequence become an accounting client of Jupp Castle.

The success of this again was through creative marketing using squeeze landing pages (Trail-Scouts), for example: http://jupp castle.co.uk/businessbreakfast

Since March a further 688 people have engaged with additional emails, created due to the success and oversubscription of the March workshops, and a further 33 attendees have booked.

So that is 1,825 people who have replied to emails, visited Jupp Castle landing pages or asked questions about the workshops, with a total of 102 workshop bookings.

In addition, the new Jupp Castle HQ website (**www.juppcastle.co.uk**) has gone from *not* being found online at all to being *no.1* on Google Searches for the Keywords: 'Accountants Hartley Wintney' and Bookkeeper 'Hartley Wintney' and on the first page of Google for 'Accountant Hampshire', 'Accountants Fleet', 'Accountants Farnborough', 'Book Keeping Hampshire', 'Book keeping Fleet' – plus many more.

The Jupp Castle website has been highly praised for its originality and creativity using many hand-drawn designs throughout, which softens the strong purples in the website. It is also reflects the fun and left field approach the Jupp Castle team like to take to business.

We made sure that we engaged a graphic designer who really understood us. A young graphic designer recently graduated from Bournemouth University, Emily Hazleton, and project manager Emma Keast, who both work at Hampshire-based Yomp Marketing were selected. This 'support local' Hampshire-based businesses really is our ethos.

Using the same original style, the new packages used hand-drawn bronze, silver and gold shields (see home page – **www.juppcastle.co.uk**) which again is an eye-catching, creative link to the 'castle' part of the Jupp Castle brand and obviously resonated with this client (see video link) – **http://youtu.be/UiF7YrRRc98**

One of the most fun pages on the website, which has received excellent feedback from potential clients wanting to find out more about Jupp Castle, is the Meet the Team page and the crowns on the team members' heads – it is quite the conversation starter and very different for an accountants website – **www.juppcastle.co.uk/meet-the-team/**

See what one of Heather's clients think about her and the fun side of Jupp Castle here: **http://youtu.be/zCyMijw4tcE**

This high Google position and creative, dynamic, new website and brand has generated unbelievable results independently of the fantastic results from the Xero workshops:

Seven website enquiries in March, 20 enquiries in April, 29 enquiries in May, 20 enquiries in June, and a staggering 43 website enquiries in July.

That is a grand total since the event of...
119 x Website enquiries
102 x Email Marketing event follow up / Workshop enquiries
Totalling 221 business enquiries since the event.

To further win clients and capitalise on this first six months of success we have created and launched a second 'Small Business Events' micro website (TrailBlazer OutPost), to optimise and capture their target market in Hampshire, Berkshire, Surrey and Dorset who are looking to network, learn and attend accountancy related educational events:
www.juppcastleevents.co.uk

So far this website has had very promising early results, and the 'Government Funding options to help Grow your Business'

Seminar that is the next event created and hosted by Jupp Castle is already nearly fully booked.

All of this activity, as you can well imagine, has resulted in a clear upsurge in turnover, new clients being regularly won, as well as selling more to the existing client base who also enjoy the monthly email newsletter, events and fun outlook from their trusted accountants, Jupp Castle.

THE AUTHOR

Richard Woods is an entrepreneur, speaker and author based in Surrey, England. He has a serious obsession with Entrepreneurship, Design and Digital Marketing.

He thinks of entrepreneurship as a sport which if you train hard at and have some natural talent for, with enough blood sweat and tears it will pay off.

He runs a large portfolio of businesses including:

- A Digital Marketing Agency Yomp Marketing
  www.yompmarketing.com,
- A Videography, Audio and Photography Company Yomp
  VAP **www.yompvap.com**
- An oil distribution business Top Up Fuels
  www.topupfuels.co.uk
- A Property / Asset Management Business Yomp Consultancy.

His latest company to launch is The Digital TrailBlazer **www.digitaltrailblazer.co.uk**, which aims to help small service sector businesses rapidly grow using cutting edge marketing techniques.

He is a frequent speaker at large business events, trade shows and seminars.

He appeared on *The Apprentice*, Series 11 (BBC1 2015)

He loves rugby, hiking and climbing, which he does with his brother and business partner Tim Woods, and father Dennis Woods.

You can keep in touch with Richard on his Blog, YouTube and Twitter:
www.digitaltrailblazer.co.uk/blog/
www.facebook.com/DigitalTrailBlazer
www.twitter.com/Richard_Woods
www.facebook.com/TheYomp

Lightning Source UK Ltd.
Milton Keynes UK
UKOW06f0251140416

272217UK00008B/125/P

9 781781 331699